D1482447

A Holy Hour with Mother Angelica

Also by Mother Angelica:

Praying with Mother Angelica
Meditations on the Rosary, the Way of the
Cross, and Other Prayers

Mother Angelica on Christ and Our Lady

Mother Angelica on Suffering and Burnout

Mother Angelica's Quick Guide to the Sacraments

Mother Angelica on Prayer and Living for the Kingdom

Mother Angelica on God, His Home, and His Angels

Mother Angelica's Practical Guide to Holiness

Mother Angelica's Answers, Not Promises

A Holy Hour with Mother Angelica

Edited by

Mary Claire Kendall and Taylor Wilson

EWTN PUBLISHING, INC.

Irondale, Alabama

EWTN Publishing, Inc.
5817 Old Leeds Road, Irondale, AL 35210

Distributed by Sophia Institute Press, Box 5284, Manchester, NH 03108.

paperback ISBN 978-1-68278-190-6
ebook ISBN 978-1-68278-191-3
Library of Congress Control Number: 2020952200

First printing

Contents

A Holy Hour with Mother Angelica

Chapter 1

"An Hour of Reparation"

So many films and plays and magazine articles today seem to take not only God's name in vain, but also take great liberties in blaspheming God and in committing sacrilege. It is crystal-clear that they have lost the concept and the reality of Who God really is.

So, we are going to have an hour of reparation. You know, we used to call them "Holy Hours." The Holy Hour was when you went to church and had a holy hour for a specific reason. During Lent you said the Stations of the Cross; throughout May and October you said the Rosary together.

What exactly does a "Holy Hour" mean? It means you dedicate an hour totally to God—praising Him, loving Him, and saying to Him, "Lord, I'm sorry that so many people don't know You, love You, or praise You."

There's one particular movie called *Hail Mary*,[1] which screened in movie houses and at universities and even in homes, was one of the worst mockeries of God's sovereign rights, the beauty of His mother, and the Incarnation of His Son. It was an abomination of desolation. Christ have mercy! The sad part is that we do not take this abomination seriously. We shrug it off, except when it comes to rights—freedom of press and freedom of expression. And

[1] Directed by Jean-Luc Godard (Sara Films, 1985).

A Holy Hour with Mother Angelica

I have to ask myself: What about God's rights and His freedom of expression? Why are we so afraid to stand tall when it comes to this? You know what the Lord said one time? "And do not be afraid of those who can kill the body but cannot kill the soul. But rather be afraid of him who is about to kill both soul and body in hell" (Matthew 10:28).

Oh, you say, "Mother, are you trying to scare us?" To which I say, I am trying to petrify you! Why? Because we have to recover our sense of awe, our sense of the majesty of God so that we do not treat God in a manner in which we would not dream of treating our neighbor or family member. Or it could be, in fact, that we are disrespectful to family and neighbors, which is why we have no regard for God. Maybe having discarded family life and that beautiful sense of each other's dignity, we have similarly lost the sense of God's dignity.

The main point of this Holy Hour, and every one following this one, is for you to luxuriate in God's presence. To forget all of your problems and all of your frustrations, and to just become aware of the awesome presence of God. I want you to listen to what is being imparted to you and to take it into your heart; I want you to have a humble heart and say, "Lord God be merciful to me, a sinner." I want all of us to bow before His Majesty and say *Mea Culpa, Mea Culpa, Mea Maxima Culpa* ("My fault, my fault, my most grievous fault").

It is in that spirit of awe and love and sense of the presence of God that I want you to listen, to pray with us, and to praise with us.

What has happened in today's world, what is happening to our society and to our minds and our hearts, is such that we seem to have lost the sense of the awesome majesty of God. Blasphemy and sacrilege do not stir us to reparation. We fail to understand how terrible it is.

What has happened to us?

I wonder sometimes how fear influences us. We seem to have fear of the world, but no fear of God. Is it a lack of prayer in our life that has made us lose that awesome fear of the Lord? We try to push Him into a corner, whereas we fear this organization or this person, or this, that, or the other thing. So, we will blaspheme the Lord rather than standing tall with Him. What is it? What is wrong with our culture?

Pray!

Imagine Our Lady, the Mother of God, as she sees John and all the apostles trying to unnail Christ from the Cross. And they let Him down with the rope. She sits on a rock and she sees up-close the terrible wounds in His hands and the terrible crown of thorns on His head. She sees His heart pierced with a lance. She sees that terrible scourging where parts of His flesh were torn away from Him. And then she looks up at the Father, she looks at her Son, and she says, "When You were born, I held you. A little babe sleeping gently. And here You are once again in my arms sleeping. I watched You grow into a man and You left Your home to share Your love. Now You have come back to me into my arms. They set You free, You talked of love and forgiveness and to love one's neighbor as oneself. Is it because of what You said that You are now in my arms lying dead? Father, please forgive them, for they have killed my only Son. I pray Your will be done, for in my arms rests my lifeless Son. In my arms rests our lifeless Son."

Let us pray a Litany of the Holy Name of Jesus:

Jesus, Son of the living God,
have mercy on us.
Jesus, Splendor of the Father,
have mercy on us.
Jesus, Brightness of eternal Light,
have mercy on us.

A Holy Hour with Mother Angelica

Jesus, King of Glory,
have mercy on us.
Jesus, Sun of Justice,
have mercy on us.
Jesus, Son of the Virgin Mary,
have mercy on us.
Jesus, most amiable,
have mercy on us.
Jesus, most admirable,
have mercy on us.
Jesus, the mighty God,
have mercy on us.
Jesus, Father of the world to come,
have mercy on us.
Jesus, angel of great counsel,
have mercy on us.
Jesus, most powerful,
have mercy on us.
Jesus, most patient,
have mercy on us.
Jesus, most obedient,
have mercy on us.
Jesus, meek and humble of heart,
have mercy on us.
Jesus, Lover of Chastity,
have mercy on us.
Jesus, our Lover,
have mercy on us.
Jesus, God of Peace,
have mercy on us.
Jesus, Author of Life,
have mercy on us.

Jesus, Model of Virtues,
have mercy on us.
Jesus, zealous for souls,
have mercy on us.
Jesus, our God,
have mercy on us.
Jesus, our Refuge,
have mercy on us.
Jesus, Father of the Poor,
have mercy on us.
Jesus, Treasure of the Faithful,
have mercy on us.
Jesus, good Shepherd,
have mercy on us.
Jesus, true Light,
have mercy on us.
Jesus, eternal Wisdom,
have mercy on us.
Jesus, infinite Goodness,
have mercy on us.
Jesus, our Way and our Life,
have mercy on us.
Jesus, joy of the Angels,
have mercy on us.
Jesus, King of the Patriarchs,
have mercy on us.
Jesus, Master of the Apostles,
have mercy on us.
Jesus, Teacher of the Evangelists,
have mercy on us.
Jesus, Strength of Martyrs,
have mercy on us.

Jesus, Light of Confessors,
have mercy on us.
Jesus, Purity of Virgins,
have mercy on us.
Jesus, Crown of all Saints,
have mercy on us.

Of course, it is imperative that we dispense of the smokescreen about Catholic devotion to Mary versus a non-Catholic's eclipsing of devotion to Our Lady. Apropos of which, I never cease to be amazed that we fail to understand the Immaculate Conception. It seems evident to me that God was so obliged to create a creature who was never in the power of the enemy—not even for a second—in order to be the vehicle for His Son to come into the world.

The sweetest thing about the miracle of the Marriage of Cana is where Our Lady said that one thing, the most important to remember: "Do whatever He tells you." She seemed undaunted by His reply: "What's that to you and me?" She looked at the steward and said, "Well, why don't you 'do whatever He tells you'?" (John 2:4-5).

I ask you to remember that each of us is our brother's keeper. It may be hard sometimes, but we *are* our brother's keeper. That means we are also the keeper of our brother Jesus. So, if He is maligned and blasphemed, if the Eucharist is watered-down and not taken seriously and looked upon as maybe just a symbol or whatever else, stand tall, and say "My Jesus reigns in the Eucharist, and I believe that with my whole heart, mind and soul." Be not afraid of what men say, for it is often like a puff of wind. And the Lord Jesus said once that "the opinions of man mean nothing to me." Well, we cannot live on those opinions because they come and go. I want you to stand tall for Jesus, and to be full of zeal and joy, and not be obnoxious but be ready to say "I believe in the Lord Jesus Christ."

"An Hour of Reparation"

Hail Mary, full of grace, blessed are you among women and blessed is the fruit of thy womb, Jesus. Holy Mary, Mother of God, pray for us now and at the hour of our death. Amen.

I ask Our Lady to be with us, to intercede for all those who blaspheme; for those who commit sacrileges; for those who have gone headlong in the wrong direction; for those who do not see the signs of the times. "God will not be mocked" (Galatians 6:7). So think before you act and think before you say something about the Lord. And those of you who take His name in vain under the guise of being manly, remember that the One Whose name you take in vain died an ignominious death on the Cross for your name.

I love you. But remember, God loves you an awful lot. You will never, never know how much. So, I love you, and God bless.

Chapter 2

"Abandonment to the Will of God"

There is just so much evil in the world, all of which is well-documented in the Scriptures—including some evils that I had never even thought about. Given this circumstance, I feel very strongly that these are times of revelation, times of prophets, times when the Lord is saying to us in so very many ways, by signs and wonders, and will continue to do so, that He is going to come and separate the wheat from the chaff. And you and I have to understand and bear in mind that even though God has infinite love and infinite mercy, He is also infinitely just. And you and I must care enough for our brother, our families, our city, our nation, and our world to pray for the salvation of souls.

It is very important today that you and I straighten out our own lives and use whatever time we have, not because I think the Second Coming is imminent, but to be attentive to the signs that God is going to start giving us that say to each one of us, "I am here. I am hurt. I want you to come home. I want you to be holy. I want you to stop sinning."

And, because of the special moment we find ourselves in—and I think we live in perilous times—I wanted to make a Holy Hour. It will be different perhaps than what we used to have in church, but nonetheless powerful.

A Holy Hour with Mother Angelica

Let us pray.

In the name of the Father, and of the Son, and of the Holy Spirit. Amen.

Lord God, we just put this Holy Hour in Your hands. We ask that You give us the light and the courage and strength to say what comes from You, Lord. We ask that, as this Holy Hour is dedicated to abandonment, we may learn to abandon ourselves to Your will, to Your love, to Your wisdom, to Your providence, and Your sovereign rights. So, Lord, we place this Hour in the arms and the heart of Your Son's Mother. We ask her protection, her guidance, and her inspiration, that Thy Spirit may come through clearly and powerfully. We ask this all in Thy holy name, Jesus. Amen.

I want to share about abandonment. We define the word *abandonment* because the word in many times in the world has meant "to give up, to abandon," as opposed to meaning "abandonment to God's Divine Will." I think sometimes we do not understand that God's wisdom is so far above our own. I do not even think we need to be proud. I think we just need to recognize the reality of situation—that we mistakenly view God as clueless and totally unaware, perhaps asleep.

Lord God, I praise You and bless You, Father, for the glory of Your name and that You teach us how to repent. That You show us all of our sins, our failings, our weaknesses, our infidelities. If You just bring them to our mind, Lord, and give us humility to say, "Yes, I did that and I am sorry." If You could just give us that grace, then we know we would be repentant.

We ask for repentance, the great gift of repentance—so that we can receive the great gift of mercy. We need to repent, Lord, before You so that we can be forgiven. We must know we have sinned grievously against God, against our neighbors, against ourselves.

Mary, Our Mother, we ask your intercession. Sweet Mother; tender, tender Mother, we ask your intercession. Pray for us. Obtain for each one of us that grace to say, "I have sinned and I ask God's forgiveness."

Don't worry—not even about your sins. The idea is just to know them, accept them, release them, repent of them. Just give it all to God. It is a beautiful way to deepen our abandonment to God's loving will.

We are getting deeper into the necessity of repentance, the necessity of knowing ourselves and, at the same time, giving ourselves totally to God so that we understand His sovereignty over us. And we take and accept the reality of our position as children of God with great courage and strength, and we know that we are children of God. And yet there is something about abandonment that scares people. Perhaps it's a feeling of a loss of control.

God takes care of the lilies of the field and, just so, He takes care of us. But most people think that is unrealistic. How do you reconcile the two?

Let us pray the Litany to the Sacred Heart of Jesus:

Heart of Jesus, Son of the Eternal Father,
have mercy on us.
Heart of Jesus, formed by the Holy Spirit in the womb of
   the Virgin Mother,
have mercy on us.
Heart of Jesus, substantially united to the Word of God,
have mercy on us.
Heart of Jesus, of Infinite Majesty,
have mercy on us.

A Holy Hour with Mother Angelica

Heart of Jesus, Sacred Temple of God,
have mercy on us.
Heart of Jesus, Tabernacle of the Most High,
have mercy on us.
Heart of Jesus, House of God and Gate of Heaven,
have mercy on us.
Heart of Jesus, burning furnace of charity,
have mercy on us.
Heart of Jesus, abode of justice and love,
have mercy on us.
Heart of Jesus, full of goodness and love,
have mercy on us.
Heart of Jesus, abyss of all virtues,
have mercy on us.
Heart of Jesus, most worthy of all praise,
have mercy on us.
Heart of Jesus, king and center of all hearts,
have mercy on us.
Heart of Jesus, in whom are all treasures of wisdom and
    knowledge,
have mercy on us.
Heart of Jesus, in whom dwells the fullness of divinity,
have mercy on us.
Heart of Jesus, in whom the Father was well pleased,
have mercy on us.
Heart of Jesus, of whose fullness we have all received,
have mercy on us.
Heart of Jesus, desire of the everlasting hills,
have mercy on us.
Heart of Jesus, patient and most merciful,
have mercy on us.

Heart of Jesus, enriching all who invoke Thee,
have mercy on us.
Heart of Jesus, fountain of life and holiness,
have mercy on us.
Heart of Jesus, propitiation for our sins,
have mercy on us.
Heart of Jesus, loaded down with opprobrium,
have mercy on us.
Heart of Jesus, bruised for our offenses,
have mercy on us.
Heart of Jesus, obedient to death,
have mercy on us.
Heart of Jesus, pierced with a lance,
have mercy on us.
Heart of Jesus, source of all consolation,
have mercy on us.
Heart of Jesus, our life and resurrection,
have mercy on us.
Heart of Jesus, our peace and our reconciliation,
have mercy on us.
Heart of Jesus, victim for our sins
have mercy on us.
Heart of Jesus, salvation of those who trust in Thee,
have mercy on us.
Heart of Jesus, hope of those who die in Thee,
have mercy on us.
Heart of Jesus, delight of all the Saints,
have mercy on us.

What is so important to one's prayer life is the Eucharist. It says, "I am the Bread of Life." You know we fast from earthly bread, from earthly attachments, and we need to be detached also from our weaknesses and our attachments to sin. But Jesus is the real bread that comes down from Heaven. He is our food. He is our strength. Without Him, we have no life.

I would like to leave you with words from the Lord, which are that "we are only earthenware jars that hold a treasure" (2 Corinthians 4:7). What is the treasure? Well, the treasure is grace in your heart, from the whole Trinity. And it says here — to clarify — that overwhelming grace comes from God, not from us. And we are in difficulties on all sides, but we are never cornered. We may have no answers to our problems, but we never despair.

So why does God give us all this grace and His awesome presence? We, with our unveiled faces, reflect like mirrors the brightness of the Lord. And all of us grow brighter and brighter as we are transformed into the image that we reflect. It's like when you are looking into a clear pond: you see yourself, but that image never becomes you. With God's grace, however, we actually become the image we reflect. And, He says, that is the work of the Spirit Who is the Lord.

And so you and I have been given great work from God — the greatest work in the world — and that is cooperation. This earthenware jar becomes like God's — strong, holy, bright. And that's what abandonment is all about, you see. It is emptying myself of me and being filled with Jesus. It is not easy, but it was not easy for Him. It's not difficult, though it is humiliating, because we think we are pretty hot stuff when in fact we are earthenware jars, full of cracks. But Jesus loves our little cracked jars. I think we should substitute here that "earthenware jar" means "a crackpot." We are all little crackpots! I had a crackpot when I was a kid, a little cup it was, and I would drink from that cup. It just kind of fit in my hand. It was all cracked, but I loved that little cup.

You and I are God's little cups, and He loves us and He keeps filling us with His love and His grace.

Lord Jesus, I give You my family tonight with all my heart. I thank You for the family You have given me tonight. And I pray that one day we will all be transformed into that image that we so dimly reflect now. And we just want to be like You, Jesus. We are so far from You that we get disgruntled and discouraged and disheartened. But look upon our pride with mercy. Make us humble and make us know the difference between humility and discouragement. Lord, sometimes we take one for the other, and they are worlds and poles apart. So, Lord Jesus, we just place ourselves and abandon ourselves to You with all of our problems, in all of our sins, and with all of our loved ones and our families, and all of those we worry about, and we just give it to You, Lord. It's just too much for us to handle; we just give them all to You. We ask Your paternal blessing.

Chapter 3

"Resisting Temptation"

This Holy Hour is devoted to resisting temptation. I want to read to you Matthew 4:1-11. I will not read the entire passage, but there is a very important aspect of this Scripture reading. Jesus is being led by the Spirit into the wilderness; we have to keep that in mind, because He is being led by the Spirit to be tempted.

The first temptation of Jesus was when the devil said to the Lord, "If you are the Son of God, tell these stones to be turned into loaves of bread." At this point Jesus was tempted through His memory. I want you to understand that Jesus purified our memory, intellect, and will, because He was tempted in the same ways we are tempted. First, he was tempted through His memory. Can you imagine yourself fasting for forty days? Why, at the concept of food, you would begin to smell fresh bread. The hunger would be phenomenal. The idea of somebody planting this into your memory — bread — and bread has many aspects that would be extremely attractive to Jesus at this point. He would remember the taste, He would remember the odor. He would remember how it felt to eat bread and how filling it can be. In those days they had really filling bread; they didn't have the kind of bread that we have today. They had good thick bread that was very nourishing. So the enemy appeals to His memory, and the Lord said, "Man does not live by bread alone but on every word that comes from the mouth of God." You are tempted in your memory, too. Today, it is the memory that is most tempted, along with the imagination, too. That is the faculty of the enemy. So, he brings all kinds of pictures: lustful pictures, gluttonous pictures, greedy pictures, everything imaginable to attract you to himself, into the world and into the flesh.

That one temptation that Jesus had in His memory — it didn't work. So, the enemy turned to the intellect of Jesus, and he said, "Look, if you are the Son of God, throw Yourself down from this temple." Pride is in the intellect, and the enemy was trying to instill within the heart of Jesus a proud thought: presumption. The devil tempted Jesus to think, "I will be great. All the people will see Me up at the temple and they will look and say, 'Oh, He's going to fall' but instead, I will gently come down. Then they will believe I am the Son of God.' Pride, presumption.

So, the enemy tempted the intellect of Jesus. We are tempted in our intellect a lot today. We proudly think, "I will not serve. I will not serve. No one is going to tell me what to do or how to do it." So, our intellect is tempted. Jesus said He would put His angels in charge to support you in case you hurt your foot against a stone. Right away, Jesus turned to the Father and said, "No, I won't do that." In doing this, Jesus increases in our hearts the virtue of hope, because when He overcame the temptation of His memory, He gave us the virtue of hope. And He increases our faith, by relying totally on God's providence. That is how He overcame this temptation of the intellect. We must remember, "I need Jesus, He will take care of me. I trust in Him."

And now we see the greatest temptation of Jesus. "Next, he [the devil] took Him to a high mountain, and He saw kingdoms in the world and all its splendor. And [the devil] said, 'You see, I will give You all of this if You fall at my feet and worship me.'" What was the devil after? The will of Jesus. He wanted Jesus to turn away from the Father and give His will to Satan. And that is what happens to us today. The enemy wants your will. He wants you to bow down to him and he will get you, one way or another, unless you cling to Jesus and the Father. And so Jesus said, "You must worship the Lord your God and serve Him alone."

Jesus gave to you and me great power in our will to say no. You see people with weak wills today because they are so embroiled in passion and permissiveness and gluttony and everything imaginable. They just cannot say no, either to the world or the flesh or Satan. And remember when Jesus overcame all three temptations in all three of His faculties, He gave you and me the courage and the strength by the Word, which shows how powerful the Word is.

Lord God, Father of Heaven and earth, I praise You and bless You. Lord, Thou art great, and Thou alone art holy. Thou alone art God, and God alone art sovereign. And so I give You my memory. Lord, implant within that memory hope and courage that I may say no and take out of it all resentments and guilts and anger toward my brother, and any unforgiving spirit with which I may be filled. And Lord, look into my intellect and give me faith that I may never lose hope and be presumptuous. That I may always believe Thy words and use Thy Word to overcome the temptations in my life. Lord, give me that grace to follow Thee all the days of my life, that my will and Your will may be one. That I too may be as a gentle breeze that, united to You, the very breath of God, may always walk in Your path. That I may say yes to every inspiration. That Thy Word in Scripture may be my protection. I ask Mary, Our Mother, to help us, to give us strength and courage, to allow us to say, as she said without hesitancy, "*Fiat*—Be it done to me according to Thy will." I ask this in the name and the power of Jesus. Amen.

A Holy Hour with Mother Angelica

Let us pray the Litany of the Most Precious Blood of Jesus Christ.

God, the Father of Heaven,
have mercy on us.
God, the Son, Redeemer of the world,
have mercy on us.
God, the Holy Spirit,
have mercy on us.
Holy Trinity, One God,
have mercy on us.
Blood of Christ, only-begotten Son of the Eternal
    Father,
save us.
Blood of Christ, Incarnate Word of God,
save us.
Blood of Christ, of the New and Eternal Testament,
save us.
Blood of Christ, falling upon the earth in the Agony,
save us.
Blood of Christ, shed profusely in the Scourging,
save us.
Blood of Christ, flowing forth in the Crowning with
    Thorns,
save us.
Blood of Christ, poured out on the Cross,
save us.
Blood of Christ, price of our salvation,
save us.
Blood of Christ, without which there is no forgiveness,
save us.
Blood of Christ, Eucharistic drink and refreshment
    of souls,
save us.

Blood of Christ, stream of mercy,
save us.
Blood of Christ, victor over demons,
save us.
Blood of Christ, courage of Martyrs,
save us.
Blood of Christ, strength of Confessors,
save us.
Blood of Christ, bringing forth Virgins,
save us.
Blood of Christ, help of those in peril,
save us.
Blood of Christ, relief of the burdened,
save us.
Blood of Christ, solace in sorrow,
save us.
Blood of Christ, hope of the penitent,
save us.
Blood of Christ, consolation of the dying,
save us.
Blood of Christ, peace and tenderness of hearts,
save us.
Blood of Christ, pledge of eternal life,
save us.
Blood of Christ, freeing souls from purgatory,
save us.
Blood of Christ, most worthy of all glory and honor,
save us.

Let us pray. Almighty and eternal God, You have appointed Your only-begotten Son the Redeemer of the world, and willed to be appeased by His Blood. Grant we beg of You, that we may worthily adore this price of our salvation, and through its power be safeguarded from the evils of the present life, so that we may rejoice in its fruits forever in Heaven. Through the same Christ our Lord. Amen.

We have learned some beautiful things about the Lord's economy in the spiritual life. How He works with us—that is important to know, so that when things happen, it is not shocking, surprising or disheartening. We know that Jesus was tempted in His memory, His intellect, and His will. We know that we must resist temptation. We must not put ourselves in a position to be tempted. So, if you have a drinking problem, you are not going to sit in front of a quart of whiskey. You need to know by past experience—"I have fallen before. I had better not go there." But then, we also know that when we are tempted, we can turn it, as God wants it to be turned, into good. Isn't that wonderful? I can confound the enemy. It is like an ant making a big elephant fall flat on his face. And that is what Jesus wants you and me to do. To show, to manifest the power of God in our weakness—*in our weakness*, because He loves us so much and He wants us to overcome these weaknesses so that the brightness of Jesus will become brighter and brighter as we are turned into the image we will reflect. And when we get to the Kingdom, we will realize just exactly what beautiful things have happened in our lives because we had the ability to say no.

A priest's blessing is very powerful. The priest says, "May Almighty God bless you, in the name of the Father, the Son, and the Holy Spirit. Amen."

There is great power in that blessing. It renews within your heart your Baptism. It increases grace in our souls. And, most of all, it does what we talked about—it gives you the power to resist temptation. It gives us the power to say no to the enemy and yes to God. Remember that every time you say no to the enemy, you have said yes to God. That is so important to know. It is a very positive aspect of temptation. You have made a choice. You have said, "Jesus, I prefer You to myself. I prefer You to the world. I prefer You to every comfort and every single pleasure I could ever have. I prefer You." That is why the angels rejoice—because when a sinner repents, he says no to the enemy and yes to God. Now, all of Heaven, *all of Heaven*, rejoices.

So, make Heaven happy, will ya? And before you go to bed this evening, ask the Lord not to put you to the test, as Our Father encourages us to ask.

However, when you are put to the test, pray that you may persevere. Say yes to God and no to the enemy, and understand that all of Heaven rejoices with you when you do that.

I love you.

Chapter 4

"Love and Reparation"

My wish for this Holy Hour is that you would offer this hour of prayer for the salvation of souls, for our families, for our loved ones, for our health, for all the intentions and needs that you have. But also remember the needs of the world. Pray that Our dear Lord will have mercy upon us as we commit sins upon sins, nation upon nation, wars upon wars. So, let's offer this Holy Hour in reparation and love and in the spirit of penance so that we understand our part of the sins of the world. We ask Jesus to forgive us.

Get your Bibles, and we're going to talk about love.

As we speak of love, I want you to think also of the people you don't love and why. And I want you, before this Holy Hour is finished, to forgive them and forgive yourself so that we can lift our hearts and minds up to the Lord with hearts that are pure and uncontaminated by any hatred or dislike or anything that keeps us from really growing in this marvelous virtue.

In the thirteenth chapter of John, the Lord said that He gave us a new commandment. I would imagine the Ten Commandments were a little abrasive in those days, as they are to some people today. The concept of a new commandment—"Oh, it must be something so much better or easier," they thought. The word *new* kind of makes you buy anything—it's new. You may have bought it for years, but now it's *new*, it may have one different ingredient in it but it's *new* and so you buy it.

The Lord came up with something, I am sure, that they did not really expect. He said, "I give you a new commandment." I wonder if He paused a minute, if He just sat there and looked at them. He knew what they were thinking. "Love one another," He said. Somehow, I feel they were probably quite disappointed. They wanted something bigger and greater. Something newer and greater like, "Go out and fight with your enemies." Or, "Go out and conquer the world." But He said to love one another. What was new about this commandment? Well, let's see. The Lord says, continuing, "just as I have loved you" (13:34). That's what was new about it. We love each other, but our love varies according to how we please each other. But the Lord said no, the new commandment is new because you need to love *as He loves us*.

And how does God love us? In John 17:23, He says, "May they be so one in Us so that the world will realize it was You who sent Me, and that I have loved them as much as You love Me."

First, He says "I give you a new commandment: that you love one another as I love you." So, I have to love you the same way that Jesus loves me. Well, how does Jesus love me? Now, we know. He loves us as much as the Father loves us. Do you realize what *that* means? I am to love you as much as the Father loves the Son, and the Son loves the Father. That is how much Jesus loves you and me. And that is the new commandment.

If we thought about that—even if we did so once a month—we would be surprised what a change that would make in our lives, because the Lord is saying something else here. He says here, "All men will know you are My disciples if you love one another" (John 13:35). That is the new commandment.

I want to encourage you to do that. Just pretend that for this hour you're going to just love everybody for an hour.

"Love and Reparation"

Can you do that? Can you think of your worst enemy? Can you think of this person who has just hurt you so much that you can feel it in your heart? Think of that person now. And, just for this hour, I want you really to love that person. I want you to look at him with sympathy and empathy and see him through the eyes of Jesus. Just try to put yourself inside of Jesus and do not look with your eyes, and do not hear with your ears. Look at him through the eyes of Jesus. They are very compassionate eyes, very loving eyes, very patient eyes. And I know you may have been in hurt unjustly. But so was He! You see, it's very important for this hour that you just get out of your heart and mind so that you and I can lift up this hour to the Lord and say, "Lord have mercy on us." It is so important that you love, because if you don't, then how can God have mercy on you if you haven't had mercy on your brother? It's that simple.

Lord God, I praise You and bless You this evening as we pray together. I ask You to let us kind of just live in You for this hour, so that our heart will be Your heart, our eyes Your eyes, and our voice Your voice. That those who listen, though they may have anger and resentment in their hearts, suddenly feel those bad feelings just drop away like scales off of a fish. That somehow all the things that are so important in life and cause us to be anxious and frustrated will suddenly seem very little. And that all our hurts will be smoothed over by the salve of Your love and mercy. And so, Lord, I just ask that You look upon us and give us the peace of Thy Spirit. Let Thy Spirit just calm our souls so that, with this calmness of soul, all these frustrations may run away and disappear. Let all the wisdom that is imparted this evening be soaked up like a sponge. We ask these good things in the name and the power of Jesus and Mary. Amen.

A Holy Hour with Mother Angelica

Let us read Psalm 136:

Give thanks to God, for He is good.
His love is everlasting.
Give thanks to the God of Gods.
His love is everlasting.
Give thanks to the Lord of Lords.
His love is everlasting.
He alone performs great marvels.
His love is everlasting.
His wisdom made the Heavens.
His love is everlasting.
He set the earth on the waters.
His love is everlasting.
He made the great lights.
His love is everlasting.
The sun to govern the day,
His love is everlasting.
Moon and stars to govern the night,
His love is everlasting.
He struck down the firstborn of Egypt,
His love is everlasting.
And brought Israel out of Egypt,
His love is everlasting.
With mighty hand and outstretched arm,
His love is everlasting.
He split the Red Sea,
His love is everlasting.
Led Israel through the middle,
His love is everlasting.
Drowned Pharaoh and his army,
His love is everlasting.

He led His people through the wilderness,
His love is everlasting.
He remembered us when we were down,
His love is everlasting.
And snatched us from our oppressors,
His love is everlasting.
He provides for all living creatures,
His love is everlasting.
Give thanks to the God of Heaven,
His love is everlasting.
Amen.

Let us pray a Litany of Our Lady of Loreto:

Holy Mary,
pray for us.
Holy Mother of God,
pray for us.
Holy Virgin of Virgins,
pray for us.
Mother of Christ,
pray for us.
Mother of the Church,
pray for us.
Mother of Divine Grace,
pray for us.
Mother most pure,
pray for us.
Mother most chaste,
pray for us.
Mother inviolate,
pray for us.

A Holy Hour with Mother Angelica

Mother undefiled,
pray for us.
Mother most amiable,
pray for us.
Mother most admirable,
pray for us.
Mother of Good Counsel,
pray for us.
Mother of our Creator,
pray for us.
Mother of our Savior,
pray for us.
Mother of mercy,
pray for us.
Virgin most prudent,
pray for us.
Virgin most venerable,
pray for us.
Virgin most renowned,
pray for us.
Virgin most powerful,
pray for us.
Virgin most merciful,
pray for us.
Virgin most faithful,
pray for us.
Mirror of justice,
pray for us.
Seat of wisdom,
pray for us.
Cause of our joy,
pray for us.

Spiritual vessel,
pray for us.
Vessel of honor,
pray for us.
Singular vessel of devotion,
pray for us.
Mystical Rose,
pray for us.
Tower of David,
pray for us.
Tower of ivory,
pray for us.
House of gold,
pray for us.
Ark of the Covenant,
pray for us.
Gate of Heaven,
pray for us.
Morning star,
pray for us.
Health of the Sick,
pray for us.
Refuge of sinners,
pray for us.
Comforter of the afflicted,
pray for us.
Help of christians,
pray for us.
Queen of angels,
pray for us.
Queen of patriarchs,
pray for us.

Queen of prophets,
pray for us.
Queen of apostles,
pray for us.
Queen of martyrs,
pray for us.
Queen of confessors,
pray for us.
Queen of virgins,
pray for us.
Queen of all saints,
pray for us.
Queen conceived without original sin,
pray for us.
Queen assumed into Heaven,
pray for us.
Queen of the Holy Rosary,
pray for us.
Queen of families,
pray for us.
Queen of peace,
pray for us.

Let us pray. Grant, we beseech Thee, O Lord God, that we Thy servants may enjoy perpetual health of mind and body, and by the glorious intercession of the Blessed Mary, ever Virgin, be delivered from present sorrow and enjoy everlasting happiness. Through Christ Our Lord. Amen.

Chapter 5

"A Deeper Understanding of Repentance"

Repentance is one of those things that is a little difficult to understand.

We think it just means "I'm sorry," and that is enough. Because we are getting more and more independent, though, we are beginning to feel the "I will not serve" feeling. I mean saying, "No one is going to tell *me* what to do. I have to make that decision." That is true. But you take for granted that you have an enlightened conscience, and sometimes we don't always seek out an enlightened conscience as well as we should. So, if for example the Holy Father comes along and says something is missing [in our spiritual lives,] we say "Uh-uh, no, I don't go for that." Because of that attitude, and because it becomes so strong, it is very difficult for us to understand what repentance means. It is more than saying "I'm sorry." It means "I am determined not to do that again," or "I see the error of my ways," or "I see where I was wrong and I am determined that, somehow, I will avoid occasions of sin and will not do it again." "Now, I may fall but it's going to be out of weakness, not determination." So we rationalize on a very human level our faults and weaknesses — if we admit them at all – and our sins. And, we come to a position of finding it very difficult to say to anyone, let alone God, "I am sorry" and really mean it where there is some humility in our repentance. I heard someone say one time, "Ok,

I'm sorry. Now let's get on with it." We have to wonder what kind of repentance *that* is.

Now, when we talk about being repentant with regard to God, we have to have those two beautiful gifts of the Spirit: first is the fear of the Lord, which means, "I do not want to hurt my Father out of love and piety;" and the second is a deep reverence for God and my neighbor.

Without these two gifts of the Holy Spirit, it is going to be very difficult to be repentant, because the other gifts follow on them. Counsel can hardly follow fortitude if we don't have these foundations. And knowledge and wisdom and understanding can hardly become a part of our lives if we don't have these. These are foundation stones. That's why Scripture says that fear of the Lord is the beginning of wisdom, and wisdom is the last perfect gift of the Spirit. But before we can have any of those marvelous gifts of the Spirit in their fruition and grow and grow and grow, we must have a deep and constant sense of repentance. And it is not just repentance for this particular sin, or an attitude of "I've said it, now I can forget it, because God forgets it and I go on my way." We must have a continual attitude of repentance because that is bound together with humility. We must always be repentant not just for particular sins — for example, not because I did something yesterday or because I have this weakness. (I have lots of weaknesses. I am not going to get rid of them. They're going to die five minutes after I do.) I must live in a continuous state of repentance. It does not mean that every six seconds, I am striking my breast, saying, *Mea Culpa, Mea Culpa, Mea Maxima Culpa.* But it's an atmosphere, a sense, and attitude of heart that looks up to God, even when you have been seemingly good. You can go before the Blessed Sacrament or before God in your living room or in your closet or wherever you pray and immediately look up to God with repentant eyes and say "I know, Lord, I am a sinner — even on a good day. Even on a good day." You might think, "Well that sounds very depressing." Oh no—it's very freeing. Because I do not have to go and pray to try and excuse myself and go through all the rigamarole we go through trying to convince God that "I didn't mean it. I didn't do it. It wasn't my fault. I hope You understand." All this is done away with. I stand before God as a sinner, and say, "Lord, here I am. And I am sorry, but You are so wonderful." You see, without that attitude of repentance, you cannot see God's wonders and His goodness and His love. You cannot see it because you are bound up in yourself. But with an attitude of repentance, a repentant heart that is constant and continual, you can look at God and know yourself and say, "God, I am nothing. Oh, but I take such joy that You are all things."

So you see, repentance gives you that attitude of awareness of who you are and where you are and what you would be without Him. It makes you very sensitive to the least fault, but not become scrupulous. It is a combination of who you are and who He is. And we take such joy because that constant attitude of repentance makes us know that we are not worth all that trouble and thought. He alone is majestic and holy. And it causes joy in knowing that I am not holy, but He is; that I struggle and He is omnipotent; that I am weak, and He is powerful.

The joy in my heart is a peace that comes from repentance and the ultimate joy of knowing He is everything that I'm not. This is coupled with the beautiful reality that He loves me as I am. You know, if we could arrive at that little package of knowledge that I just gave you, why, we would make giant leaps in understanding this! Because I would no longer be afraid to see myself. In fact, my joy would be in seeing myself and seeing God. "Blessed are the clean of heart, for they shall see God" (see Matthew 5:8).

Lord God, make us repentant not with just that momentary repentance over some fault or sin. More than that,

A Holy Hour with Mother Angelica

Lord, give us an attitude of repentance—a deep awareness that we stand before Thee always as sinners, but glorifying Your goodness, Your love, Your compassion, Your mercy, and knowing that You love us, Lord, just as we are. Let me look at that, Lord. Let me never be discouraged, no matter how far I fall or how long I stay there. Let me always know I can rise to a totally new life and I can be reborn and renewed in Thy love, no matter *how far* I have fallen. I thank You, Lord, for Your mercy, Your love and Your goodness. Amen.

Let us pray the Litany of the Passion:

Jesus, the Eternal Wisdom,
have mercy on us.
Jesus, sold for thirty pieces of silver,
have mercy on us.
Jesus, prostrate on the ground in prayer,
have mercy on us.
Jesus, strengthened by an angel,
have mercy on us.
Jesus, in Thine Agony bathed in a bloody sweat,
have mercy on us.
Jesus, betrayed by a kiss,
have mercy on us.
Jesus, bound by the soldiers,
have mercy on us.
Jesus, forsaken by His disciples,
have mercy on us.
Jesus, brought before Ananias and Caiaphas,
have mercy on us.
Jesus, struck in the face by a servant,
have mercy on us.

"A Deeper Understanding of Repentance"

Jesus, accused by false witnesses,
have mercy on us.
Jesus, declared guilty of death,
have mercy on us.
Jesus, spat upon,
have mercy on us.
Jesus, blindfolded,
have mercy on us.
Jesus, smitten on the cheek,
have mercy on us.
Jesus, thrice denied by Peter,
have mercy on us.
Jesus, despised and mocked by Herod,
have mercy on us.
Jesus, clothed in a white garment,
have mercy on us.
Jesus, rejected for Barabbas,
have mercy on us.
Jesus, torn with scourges,
have mercy on us.
Jesus, bruised for our sins,
have mercy on us.
Jesus, esteemed by the leper,
have mercy on us.
Jesus, covered with the purple robe,
have mercy on us.
Jesus, crowned with thorns,
have mercy on us.
Jesus, struck with the reed upon the head,
have mercy on us.
Jesus, demanded for crucifixion by the Jews,
have mercy on us.

A Holy Hour with Mother Angelica

Jesus, condemned to an ignominious death,
have mercy on us.
Jesus, given to the will of Thine enemies,
have mercy on us.
Jesus, loaded with the heavy weight of the Cross,
have mercy on us.
Jesus, led to the slaughter like a sheep,
have mercy on us.
Jesus, stripped of Thy garments,
have mercy on us.
Jesus, fastened with nails to the Cross,
have mercy on us.
Jesus, reviled by the malefactors,
have mercy on us.
Jesus, promising Paradise to the repentant thief,
have mercy on us.
Jesus, commending St. John to Thy Mother as her Son,
have mercy on us.
Jesus, declaring Thyself forsaken by Thy Father,
have mercy on us.
Jesus, in Thy thirst given gall and vinegar to drink,
have mercy on us.
Jesus, obedient even to death on the Cross,
have mercy on us.
Jesus, pierced with a lance,
have mercy on us.
Jesus, taken down from the Cross,
have mercy on us.
Jesus, rising gloriously from the dead,
have mercy on us.
Jesus, ascending into Heaven,
have mercy on us.

Jesus, Our Advocate with the Father,
have mercy on us.
Jesus, sending down on Thy disciples Thy Holy Spirit,
have mercy on us.
Jesus, exalting Thy Mother above the choirs of angels,
have mercy on us.
Jesus, Who shall come to judge the living and the dead,
have mercy on us.

Let us pray. Almighty and Eternal God, who did appoint Thy Only Begotten Son, the Savior of the World, and willed to be appeased by His Precious Blood, grant that we may venerate this price of our salvation and, by its might, be so defended upon earth from the evils of this present life that in Heaven we may rejoice in its everlasting fruit. Through Christ Jesus, our Lord, who lives and reigns in the unity of the Holy Spirit with the Father, world without end. Amen.

Chapter 6

"An Hour of Healing"

There are all kinds of healing. I sometimes wonder if we are aware that you and I are healers. Oh, I do not mean in the sense we're going to heal somebody from cancer (although we can do that, too). But I mean in the sense of healing our neighbor constantly. Your life—your life of love and sacrifice and patient understanding—is a healing power for your neighbor.

Have you ever just been so distressed and so discouraged and someone calls you up and says "Hey, I'm a little worried about you! Is there something I can do?" When they do that, don't you feel kind of a warming inside? Well, that's healing. It has taken something that is disagreeable, something very painful, and poured love and compassion and concern on top. I think sometimes that you and I do not understand how powerful Jesus has made us. By the divine indwelling of the Holy Trinity, you have the power of Jesus to heal your broken brother. And you cannot excuse yourself by going on, saying, "I do not have a gift of healing." You have the gift: the gift of loving, the gift of listening, the gift of understanding.

How many times have your children done something that is very, very wrong? And they know it's wrong and you know it's wrong, but if you have been understanding with them, haven't they changed? There is nothing more beautiful than the healing that comes from forgiveness—whether you're the one forgiven or the one who forgives. There is such healing in forgiveness. You and I must forgive a thousand times a day. And we have been forgiven a million times a day!

We are in constant need of healing. The person who says, "I have no need of healing" has not the slightest idea what he's talking about. I would worry about someone like that. I mean, you could be the healthiest person in the world and be so sick in your soul, or even dead in it. There are many living corpses walking around. What does that mean? It means that inside, you're dead. Your soul is dead. You look alive—you have hands that move and feel and touch. But because you have not healed or refused to be healed by the compassionate and merciful Lord, you walk around as though dead, like whitened sepulchers filled with dead men's bones. I mean, look at the gentle Jesus today. What does He say? What do His apostles say?

In St. Peter's First Epistle, second chapter, verse twenty-three, he talks about Jesus. He says He was insulted but did not retaliate with insults. "Who, when He was reviled, did not revile." What a healing man He was. When He was tortured, He made no threats but put His trust in the righteous judge. He was bearing our faults in His own body on the Cross so that we might die to our faults and live in holiness. Think about that. Think about the Lord God, broken, insulted, torn to pieces—to heal you. Sometimes we're not even willing to smile to heal our brother. And yet, Jesus gave it all because you and I were sick, and He had mercy on us. You and I were alienated, and He brought us home. You and I find it hard to love God, the invisible Lord. So we get all wound up in the three great tempters: the flesh, the world, and the enemy. We get all bound up like a little kitten with yarn. So Jesus said, "Look, I love you this much. I love you enough to give up everything." I don't know—none of us know really—what it meant to be with the Father. We have no concept of Heaven. Oh, we talk about it, but it's not an experience yet with us. It's not an experience, so we don't fully understand what Jesus did.

You know, I heard some minister say—and it angered me to no end—he said it was not a humiliation for Jesus to become man. How you can say that? Do you know God? Do you have the slightest idea of what you are talking about? Have we gotten so proud that we have we have become the end and all so that God Himself coming down to our puny level is nothing? You see, that is really kind of a thermometer as to where we are in pride and holiness, and it's not too good. It's not too good at all.

So, you and I must exercise our healing powers. Exercise them and know that the touch of your hand is healing—to lift up a brother in the gutter; to listen to the same story one hundred times; to smile when you're in pain; to keep going when it's so very, very difficult; to keep trusting. All of these moments are beautiful healing times in your life.

One time, I really had some problems and anxieties and frustrations about walking down the streets. A woman came with her little kid, who had blond hair and blue eyes. And that child stopped and looked at me and smiled. I have never forgotten it because I found Jesus in that smile. I knew the Lord made that child smile at me and say "Angelica, it's okay. I'm with you. I'll never let you down."

Lord God, Sovereign Lord, we praise You and bless You and we acknowledge our nothingness before You and we ask for Your mercy. We ask that You give us a share in Your healing power—the power of love, the power of mercy and the gift of having a forgiving spirit so that we may heal our brother whom we have offended or who has offended us. Heal them and bring them home. We asked forgiveness for all our sins. In asking for forgiveness, we are healed. And by Your Son's wounds, we have all been healed and brought back to Your Kingdom. We ask these good things through the intercession of Mary, Our Holy Mother, in the name of Jesus Who is Lord of All. Amen.

Let us pray the Litany of the Holy Name of Jesus:

Jesus, Son of the living God,
have mercy on us.
Jesus, Splendor of the Father,
have mercy on us.
Jesus, Brightness of eternal Light,
have mercy on us.
Jesus, King of Glory,
have mercy on us.
Jesus, Sun of Justice,
have mercy on us.
Jesus, Son of the Virgin Mary,
have mercy on us.
Jesus, most amiable,
have mercy on us.
Jesus, most admirable,
have mercy on us.
Jesus, the mighty God,
have mercy on us.
Jesus, Father of the world to come,
have mercy on us.
Jesus, angel of great counsel,
have mercy on us.
Jesus, most powerful,
have mercy on us.
Jesus, most patient,
have mercy on us.

Jesus, most obedient,
have mercy on us.
Jesus, meek and humble of heart,
have mercy on us.
Jesus, Lover of Chastity,
have mercy on us.
Jesus, our Lover,
have mercy on us.
Jesus, God of Peace,
have mercy on us.
Jesus, Author of Life,
have mercy on us.
Jesus, Model of Virtues,
have mercy on us.
Jesus, zealous for souls,
have mercy on us.
Jesus, our God,
have mercy on us.
Jesus, our Refuge,
have mercy on us.
Jesus, Father of the Poor,
have mercy on us.
Jesus, Treasure of the Faithful,
have mercy on us.
Jesus, good Shepherd,
have mercy on us.
Jesus, true Light,
have mercy on us.
Jesus, eternal Wisdom,
have mercy on us.
Jesus, infinite Goodness,
have mercy on us.

Jesus, our Way and our Life,
have mercy on us.
Jesus, joy of the Angels,
have mercy on us.
Jesus, King of the Patriarchs,
have mercy on us.
Jesus, Master of the Apostles,
have mercy on us.
Jesus, Teacher of the Evangelists,
have mercy on us.
Jesus, Strength of Martyrs,
have mercy on us.
Jesus, Light of Confessors,
have mercy on us.
Jesus, Purity of Virgins,
have mercy on us.
Jesus, Crown of all Saints,
have mercy on us.

Let us pray. Lord Jesus Christ, You have said, "Ask and you shall receive; seek and you shall find; knock and it shall be opened to you"; mercifully attend to our supplications, and grant us the grace of Your most divine love, that we love You with all our hearts, and in all our words and actions, and never cease to praise You.

Make us, O Lord, to have a perpetual fear and love of Your holy name, for You never fail to govern those whom You establish in Your love. You, Who live and reign forever and ever. Amen.

Chapter 7

"An Hour of Joy: The Lord Is Risen!"

Holy Thursday during Easter Week was the time when the apostles were so excited because the Lord had risen. You and I should be just as excited, even as we make our Holy Hour, and even as we pray to the Lord. We have to have that joy in our heart and mind because as St. Paul said, had Christ not risen, our faith would be useless.

But He is risen!

He is risen in our hearts. That is the important thing. As Christians — as those who have been baptized, those of us who have been confirmed in the Spirit — we have those seven gifts that are so important in our life. As we prepare for Pentecost, we look at the risen Jesus in His glory, and we have to compare what He suffered to where He is now. That is our point of encouragement and hope, because you and I are in this valley of tears. But we have a Lord who is risen to look up to and to know that we, too, shall be risen one day, that we shall be in His Kingdom, in that Kingdom there are no tears nor pain. Everyone will love you and you will love everyone, and there will be joy and knowledge that would just boggle your mind. There is so much to look forward to that I think our present problems, as St. Paul says, are really not worth looking at compared to the glories that are to come.

That is what the risen Jesus has given us today — that's Holy Week's celebration. Because, as Christians, we have something to look forward to, and Someone to look forward to. That is the joy of this week — that our suffering (through darkness, travail and weakness of heart and mind sometimes) is somehow all worth it. That is what this week this says to me. The things we do not understand, the misunderstandings in our life, the heartaches, the physical pain, the mental pain, the spiritual pain, the pain that comes from outside, and the pain that comes deep within — everything that the Lord suffered, He said to you, "Look, this is the result. Have hope. This will happen to you, but when you die you will see Me face to face."

This is our week of hope. The Resurrection is our hope. He kept His promise. He said the Son of Man would suffer, be scourged, be crucified, and on the third day He would rise again. And He did. He did! That is your courage. That is my courage — in the Lord Jesus.

And so, you and I with all of our problems, whatever they may be — all our aches and pains — must never forget that He is risen. And even if we have not really kept all our Lenten promises and said, "Well, I really did not change in those areas that I wanted to," it's okay. At least you know that. Self-knowledge is ninety percent of the battle. Just say, "Lord, let me never forget that my whole life, even my faults and my sins, will be used by You for my good — somehow. And that, one day, all of the shackles of weakness will fall off of me like the scales from the fish, and I, too, shall rise." And you and I can arise this moment from our other self — the selfish person within me, the unforgiving person, the angry person, the frustrated person, the person who is impatient — whatever we are. He has said to us, "I am risen." Look up — this is the day that the Lord has made. You and I shall also have that day that gives our pain meaning. Today, so many are losing hope and, for example, committing suicide; they just have forgotten the Resurrection, and that He is risen. Isn't that great? He is among us. He is within us now, and in the Eucharist. He is always with us. He never, never leaves us.

"An Hour of Joy: The Lord Is Risen!"

And so I want you to have not only a very grace-filled week, but I want this Holy Hour to be one of joy for you. I want it to be one that gives you that deep realization that God wants to be risen in your heart. He wants you to look out of your eyes, speak with your voice, hear with your ears. He wants to be risen in your life. He wants this old self to die. It's painful. But you see, Jesus, too, went through the beauty of the Incarnation—that's the beauty of the Son of God becoming man.

I've said this to you before. We had the audacity in the time of the Old Testament, to look at the Lord, at Yahweh Himself, and say, "Lord, Yahweh, You ask me to be patient, but has anyone ever hurt You? Has anyone ever slapped You in the face? Have You ever suffered from impatience and ambition and hatreds? Have You ever done great good and then been ignored? Have You ever suffered from ingratitude and hunger and thirst? Have You ever been cold, Lord?" And, Our Lord would have said, "I will come down and I will suffer as no one has ever suffered. I will be hungry and thirsty. I will know what it is to be slapped in the face and to be thrown out of synagogues and to have people walk away because I have said something they do not like, and I will know what it is to suffer from jealousy and lose my friends. I will know. I will experience hunger and thirst. I will feel it because I love you."

At this point you and I do not have much to say after that, do we? I think we have a lot of excuses, complaining of "this injustice in my life." But we really do not anymore. So, we look up during Holy Week, especially, because many graces will flow to you. And all of these great feasts that we have, you want to say, "Lord, give me all the special graces that this feast gives to me and gives to the world."

Let us pray. Lord God, Risen Lord, You know You have been hungry with me and thirsty with me and You have cried with me. And now You have risen. You have overcome. And

You did it out of love. Teach me, Lord, how to love. I some-times grin and bear it because there is nothing else to do, though I might be grumbling all the way. But Your love was so intense that your poor human nature almost tore apart. But it never marred that image of Your love. Nothing ever stood between You and the Father. Unfortunately, many things stand between Thee and me. And, some are very small and insignificant. And so, Lord, as I present myself to You, lift me up and teach me how to pray, and how to love without any kind of compromise—without counting the costs. Teach me, Lord, how to rise above myself that I might be You—another Christ—to my neighbor. Amen.

Let us pray the Litany of the Love of God, composed by Pope Pius VI:

You Who are infinite love,
I love You, Lord Jesus.
You Who first loved me,
I love You, Lord Jesus.
You Who command me to love You,
I love You, Lord Jesus.
With all my heart,
I love You, Lord Jesus.
With all my soul,
I love You, Lord Jesus.
With all my mind,
I love You, Lord Jesus.
With all my strength,
I love You, Lord Jesus.
Above all possessions and honor,
I love You, Lord Jesus.
Above all pleasures and enjoyments,

"An Hour of Joy: The Lord Is Risen!"

I love You, Lord Jesus.
More than myself and all that belongs to me,
I love You, Lord Jesus.
More than all my relatives and friends,
I love You, Lord Jesus.
More than all persons and all angels,
I love You, Lord Jesus.
Above all created things in Heaven or on earth,
I love You, Lord Jesus.
Because You are the Sovereign Good,
I love You, Lord Jesus.
Because You are infinitely worthy of being loved,
I love You, Lord Jesus.
Because You are infinitely perfect,
I love You, Lord Jesus.
Even if You should try me by misfortune,
I love You, Lord Jesus.
In wealth and in poverty,
I love You, Lord Jesus.
In prosperity and in adversity,
I love You, Lord Jesus.
In health and in sickness,
I love You, Lord Jesus.
In life and in death,
I love You, Lord Jesus.
In time and in eternity,
I love You, Lord Jesus.
In union with that love, with which all the saints and all
the angels love You in Heaven,
I love You, Lord Jesus.
In union with that love with which the Blessed Virgin
Mary loves You,

A Holy Hour with Mother Angelica

I love You, Lord Jesus.

Lord Jesus, thank You for empowering me to return Your love. Thank You, Jesus, for loving me and sending me Your Holy Spirit, who empowers me to profess You as Lord, to accept Your Lordship over my whole life, to love others, and to love You. Thank You, Jesus.

Praise to You, glory to You, Lord, and I glorify You and I bless You and I praise You, because You are risen and because You are Lord. Thank You, Jesus. Amen.

Let us pray a Novena to the Holy Spirit, and especially for the gifts of the Holy Spirit.

Father, let Your Spirit come upon us with power to fill us with His gifts. Make our hearts pleasing to You and ready to do Your will. We ask this through Our Lord Jesus Christ, who lives and reigns with You in the unity of the Holy Spirit. Amen.

Chapter 8

"An Hour of Faith and Hope and Love"

During this Holy Hour, we are going to talk and pray over faith and hope in our lives.

Turn to St. John's Gospel, the twentieth chapter, and twenty-fourth verse. It's about St. Thomas. I know you have heard this a hundred times, but you know, Scripture is different than anything else you read, because no matter how often you've read a passage, the Spirit will bring something in that passage out to you that you've never understood before. That's the gift of understanding in operation: something is always new about the Scriptures because God is infinite. We never even begin to tap the wisdom and understanding of God.

In this passage, we would like to bring out, perhaps, some things that you have never thought about before. So, let's go over this for a minute. St. Thomas, called the Twin, was not with the apostles when Jesus appeared. When they told him, "We have seen the Lord," he famously answered (and here I am paraphrasing), "Unless I see the holes that the nails made in His hands and can put my finger into the holes, and unless I can put my hand into His side, I refuse to believe." Belief is an act of the will. "I am not going to believe," said Thomas. He had made a decision. You see, there's one thing you and I have to examine ourselves on. We make decisions sometimes. We make decisions about God's promises. We make decisions about what God does in our lives. We make decisions, for example saying, "I am going to go this far and I am not going to go any further. And, Lord, You can take me this far. But, really, do not ask me to go up another notch." As a result, you put limits on God.

And that is exactly what Thomas did. He said, "I refuse to believe." He put a limit. He said, "I am going to believe provided, Lord, that You do these things." And I bet you are saying to yourselves, "Oh, I'd never do that." But we do it all the time! You do it. I do it. What do we do? Well, many times, we will say, "Lord, I want to give You everything. I want to be a saint." But when one hard thing comes along that goes against our grain, we say, "I don't really think God wants that of me." So we set a limit. Thomas set a limit. When we talk about faith and hope, we wonder why we do not grow — but look at your limits. What limits have you placed on God? Then we see very quickly why we are not making these giant leaps of faith and hope.

Well, eight days passed for Thomas. The Lord made Thomas wait eight solid days, and all during those eight days Thomas kept hearing the apostles say, "The Lord is risen. The Lord is risen."

Now, we begin to see that in the beginning, when Thomas refused, when he made an act of his will, he lacked faith. But after waiting so long, he also began to lack hope. Faith allows you to see God, and hope allows you to wait. We all want to be holy. You know, one day I once said, "Lord, will I ever wake up patient? Will I ever wake up gentle or compassionate? Will I forever have to work on it?" Well, I would imagine that the Lord nodded His head and said, "Yes, but you have to wait."

Hope gives you joy while you wait; it gives you confidence while you wait; it gives you trust while you wait. As the Lord begins to show you your ups and your downs — up and down: you are good today; you are not too hot tomorrow; you are good today, and so on — you get so tired of that roller coaster. And hope says, "No, I am on the way. The Lord loves me and I have His grace within me."

Well, you can see how poor Thomas began to lose a lot of hope. The more enthusiastic the apostles were, the more the Lord appeared to other people. And you and I have felt that. Haven't you heard somebody say, "The Lord said to me this morning…" and you say, "Oh?" Maybe the first time you believed it, thinking, "Well, maybe He'll talk to me tomorrow morning." But, if day after day passes and the Lord, as far you're concerned, has not said a word to you, and you hear people saying "the Lord said this, the Lord said that," you begin to say, "Oh really?" So, what do you do? You shut it out. You say, "Well, He does not say anything to me. Why? He doesn't say anything to me." So, we begin to lose hope. You see? You do it. I do it. We think that if it does not happen to us, it does not exist.

We need to watch that carefully. You know, I am fully convinced the Lord has always purposefully made me friends with mystics. I'm not a mystic. I go the hard way: through faith. And yet, I am grateful for that. I am very grateful the Lord has surrounded me with holy people, because I cannot imagine what I would be without the them, so I am grateful. I will never have their mystical experiences. It's not my way. God deals with me differently — so He does with you. You don't need to envy the apostles here, as I would imagine Thomas did. He didn't see it, and so for him it didn't exist. All of them were a bunch of crazy emotional men.

Let's see what happened.

Well, after the eighth day, the doors were closed, and Jesus came and stood among them. And you know what He said. He said the same thing He wants to say to me and to you: "Peace be with you."

Having the virtues of faith and hope are when you have the assurance that the promise will be fulfilled — that you *see* Jesus in the present moment, but you *have* Jesus in the present moment. You don't need to wait for Heaven. When you begin to lose faith and hope, though, you lose that most precious of all God's gifts: peace.

Do you ever wonder why the Lord said, "Peace be with you"? It is because peace is what they had lost. They did not see God in His sufferings, they saw a man. You and I don't see God in our sufferings. We see those who caused them, or we see ourselves. Jesus suddenly became a prophet — they questioned if He *was* the Son of God. They could not see God in suffering. You and I have the same problem. We just cannot see God in our sufferings — not only those sufferings caused by other things, but also the sufferings caused by our own faults and failings. We want to be so holy, but we rebel so often.

Well let's see what happened next. The Lord looked to Thomas and He said, "Put your finger here." The Lord had heard Thomas. The Lord hears you and me when we start mouthing off. "Here are My hands," the Lord said. Can you imagine the look on Thomas' face? And the Lord said, "Give Me your hand and put it into My side; and do not doubt, but believe" (John 20:27).

And Jesus, you know, He was so sweet. Then Thomas said, "My Lord and my God." He knew Jesus was God, for He had suddenly jumped from prophet to God in the mind of Thomas.

The Lord said, "Thomas, blessed are those who have not seen and yet believed" (John 20:29). So, the sufferings you have are permitted by God — that's faith. That you are suffering with God and in God is hope. There is value to suffering. When you lose the value of your pain and suffering and heartache, you despair, and despair is the opposite of hope.

Lord God, we are people who are very much like Thomas all of our lives. We lack faith and we lack hope. We lose courage very quickly, Lord. Our pride prevents us from finding joy and self-knowledge in sufferings at the present moment. So, although faith is the threshold that allows me to see You in the present moment, give me hope, too — an increase of hope that would allow me to embrace You in the present moment. Lord, I believe. Help my unbelief. Lord, I hope You will keep me from discouragement. Amen.

Let us pray the Litany of Our Lady of Perpetual Help:

God the Father of Heaven,
have mercy on us.
God the Son, Redeemer of the World,
have mercy on us.
God the Holy Spirit,
have mercy on us.
Holy Trinity, One God,
have mercy on us.
Holy Mary,
pray for us.
Holy Mother of God,
pray for us.
Holy Virgin of Virgins,
pray for us.
Queen conceived without the stain of Original Sin,
pray for us.
Queen of the Most Holy Rosary,
pray for us.
Our Lady of Perpetual Help,
pray for us.
Mother of Perpetual Help, whose very name inspires
confidence,
pray for us.
That I may love God with all my heart,
pray for us.

A Holy Hour with Mother Angelica

That I may in all things conform my will to that of your
Divine Son,
pray for us.
That I may always shun sin, the only real evil,
pray for us.
That I may always remember my last stand,
pray for us.
That I may often and devoutly receive the Sacraments,
pray for us.
That I may avoid every proximate occasion of sin,
pray for us.
That I may generously pardon my enemies,
pray for us.
That I may be strong against my own inconstancy,
pray for us.
That I may not delay my conversion from day to day,
pray for us.
That I may lead others to love and serve God,
pray for us.
That I may live and die in the friendship of God,
pray for us.
When I am assailed by the evil spirits,
pray for us.
When I am tempted by the allurements of a deceitful
world,
pray for us.
When I am struggling against the inclinations of my own
corrupt nature,
pray for us.
When the loss of my senses shall warn me that my earthly
end is at hand,
pray for us.

When the thought of my approaching dissolution shall fill
me with fear and terror,
pray for us.
When at the decisive hour of death, the evil spirit will
endeavor to plunge my soul into despair,
pray for us.
When the priest of God shall give me his last absolution
and his final blessing,
pray for us.
When the world will vanish from my side and my heart
will cease to beat,
pray for us.
When my soul will appear before its Sovereign Judge,
pray for us.
When the irrevocable sentence will be pronounced,
pray for us.
When I will be suffering purification in Purgatory and
sighing for the vision of God,
pray for us.

Almighty and merciful God, Who in order to help the human race You have willed that the Blessed Virgin Mary become the Mother of Your Only Begotten Son, grant, O Father, we beseech You, that by her intercession we may avoid the contagion of sin and serve Thee with a pure heart, through Jesus Christ, Our Lord. Amen.

Let us pray the Novena of the Holy Spirit:

Father, let Your Spirit come upon us with power to fill us with His gifts. Make our hearts pleasing to You and ready to do Your will. We ask this through Our Lord Jesus Christ, who lives and reigns with You in the unity of the Holy Spirit. Amen.

A Holy Hour with Mother Angelica

Holy Michael, the Archangel, defend us in battle. Be our protection against the wickedness and snares of the devil. May God rebuke him, we humbly pray, and do thou, O Prince of the Heavenly Host, by Divine Power thrust into Hell Satan and all the other evil spirits who wander through the world seeking the ruin of souls. Amen.

The blessing of a priest is so powerful. He will say, "May Almighty God bless you, in the name of the Father, the Son, and the Holy Spirit. Amen."

When a priest blesses you, it is Jesus Who blesses you. We have always wished we were with the apostles or the children when the Lord placed His hand on their heads and blessed them. If you have any problems, if you have any kind of distress, especially interior distress, if you have anything at all—the power of the priest's blessing can take all of that away, because it is the blessing of Jesus.

Remember that in the present moment faith allows you to see Jesus. And that's difficult sometimes. People get in the way; things get in the way. Faith penetrates. It's like a laser it just goes right through. It takes away all the veneer, the clouds, the issues, and says, "God permits this. God ordains this, or God wants this." Then, hope comes along right after, and says, "Yes, I accept it. There is good in this." It may be very painful, but then a beautiful thing happens. Love comes right in and embraces faith and hope and says "I love you." And we see how wonderful Jesus is. See, Jesus is wonderful to know—that He's going to bring good out of it is tremendous. But unless you say "I love you" in this, there would be something lacking. So these are stepping stones. Remember to say, "I believe, I know He loves me and I accept that love and respond to that love." And sometimes saying this Novena to the Holy Spirit is an act of love. We should say, "Love, teach me how to love with Your love." If we could just sometimes sit down and meditate and absorb the love of Jesus, the love of the Father—that's His Spirit. It's that simple, and if you can't think of anything, don't worry about it, God doesn't need your thoughts. He needs your love. Just imagine for a moment the love that is constantly flowing between Father and Son and then penetrates you. That's the beauty of His Resurrection.

Chapter 9

"An Hour of Trusting in God"

We are going to talk about faith and hope. There is a great passage in Scripture that, to me, is phenomenal. I meditate on it at least once a day—sometimes more depending on the day. It's the twenty-first chapter of John. I want you to look at it. Every time I look at it, I get something new. This was just after the Resurrection and the disciples, God bless them, are hungry. There are times when you are so filled with spiritual food or the excitement of the day that you do not feel physically hungry. Have you ever noticed how you lose your appetite? Well, these apostles didn't, I'm happy to say. So after seeing the Lord a few days, well, nature set in. And Peter said, "Look, I'm hungry." Another replied, "So am I," and they decided they'd go fishing. So Thomas went, Peter went, and Nathaniel and James and John as well.

Now this is the point I want you to listen to, because all of you who feel such failures or feel there's so much to do and you are not able or competent to do it, I want you to listen to this. The Scripture tells us it was daylight, so they had been out fishing all evening, and all through the early morning. There stood Jesus on the shore that morning, but they did not know it was Jesus. They were kind of far out on the water, but they saw a figure on the beach. And the stranger—you have to realize now—just take away the word "Jesus" because they didn't know it was Jesus. And, this strange figure said, "Have you caught anything, friends?" Well, that was a dangerous question. There is a stranger on the shore and you are wet, you are cold, you're hungry, and you have failed. I want you to look at all three physical things. You're wet, cold, hungry. And, you have failed. You've failed totally in supplying for any of these needs, and then some perfect stranger maybe fifty to sixty feet away from you says, "Have you caught anything?" In other words, He put salt on the wound. He wants you to feel that total helplessness. And you see, you and I sometimes fight against that feeling. The stranger wanted somebody to say what Peter said, which was "No." You know, in the economy of God exists a necessity of reaching that level where we are willing not only to know we have failed, but to admit it. So Peter said, "No."

Have you ever wondered why the Lord chose these men? Because actually they were ignorant fishermen, or ignorant laymen. Why didn't Jesus, Who wanted to found a whole new Church, go to the men who knew the Church? The Scribes, the Pharisees, Sadducees, the lawyers, the high priests? Why did He not get them together and give them a lot of grace and say, "Boys, we're going to start something new"? Why did He go and pick ignorant laymen with so many faults? As we have learned, they were not even good fishermen.

Why? You are going to learn right now. You are going to learn the qualities that Jesus demanded and got from these men that He did not get from anyone else, and that I think He can get from you, too.

The first quality is honesty, or integrity. Peter said no; no excuses. I would have said "I didn't go out fishing, I went outside to meditate!" I wouldn't have admitted I went out to fishing. Today, we would have said something else to make it nice. But Peter said "No. I didn't catch anything. I failed." That's the first quality of someone who can do great things for God: being able to admit, "I blew it."

Now, the stranger says something else. (Remember, this is a stranger. Don't think "Jesus" for now.) The stranger says, "Throw the net out to the starboard side and you will find something." Wrong side of boat, wrong time of day and wrong place. You are talking to commercial fishermen. They made a living catching fish. Now a stranger asked them to do what? Three ridiculous things. And now we see another quality, The first in saying, "no" we saw humility and in the second we see obedience. To a perfect stranger! What did he have to lose? It was so ridiculous. The water was shallow, it was dawn, and they had to take all the gear away from the ship and throw nets—and they did it. But they only did it after they admitted failure.

Humility was the foundation, and then God told them to do a ridiculous thing. And, suddenly, there were so many fish in that net so quickly they couldn't haul it in. Then John recognizes Jesus and says, "It is the Lord."

And, now we're going to see another quality in Peter. Here we find out why Peter was chosen to be head of the Church of God. We learn that he had humility, he had obedience, and now what does he manifest? Repentant love. Do you realize what you would have done? I know what I would've done if I denied the Lord three times and somebody said "It's Jesus." I might have just kind of sunk down in the boat and covered my face in what would have seemed to me to be repentance. But it really would have been pride.

We see that Peter was willing to accept the total and absolute forgiveness of Jesus. And he wanted Jesus to know again and again how sorry he was. And so, what does he do? He throws himself into the water as soon as he hears it's Jesus. He didn't say "Oh Lord," like he did before when they caught another big haul of fish and he had said, "Lord depart from me, I am a sinful man." But now, after he had really fallen and had humbled himself, he acquired the humility he needed to convert his brother. As Jesus said, he is now a new man. You see, he had changed. You and I kind of slink into the bottom of our boats when we sin. We cannot believe that Jesus forgives and forgets. That's why we do not take risks. We say, "Oh, Lord, I am not worthy." Well *who* is worthy? What are you waiting for? Do you think God has bad taste? What? It is your unworthiness that attracts God. It is our stupidities that attract God. We do not know what things can and cannot be done, just like Peter, who did not know you could catch fish at that time of day. He just did it. So we have to know in this beautiful passage how to just do it.

And another thing you have to learn here is the beauty of God blessing our human nature. With all that power, with all those miracles, and the miracle of His presence, He cooked breakfast for His apostles. You and I do not have a concept of God cooking breakfast. We really don't. We would have said, "Look, I am the Lord God. I am risen from the dead. Why are you thinking of food at this moment?" But he had the charcoal fire. I always wondered where He got the charcoal. He had fish. Not only did He forgive and forget, He prepared a meal to celebrate.

When you feel that things cannot be done or you are not able to do them, read this chapter. There is a wealth of God's providence in it. It is a story very much like the woman who touched Jesus' garment and He felt the power leave Him:

Lord God, give us the humility of Peter, the obedience of Peter and his repentant love, so that we, too, can trust You in the present moment knowing that many times we are asked to do the ridiculous—so that You, Lord God, can do the miraculous. We wish to adhere to Your will. And, Lord, we wish to listen to Your presence, Your silent presence that comes to us so vividly and so strongly in the demands of the present moment. We ask this grace for all of us, so that we too may be humble of heart, obedient unto death, and ever-aware of our weaknesses while trusting in Your love. Amen.

Let us pray a Litany Prayer to Jesus:

You Who are infinite love,
I love You, Lord Jesus.
You Who did first love me,
I love You, Lord Jesus.
You, Who command me to love You,
I love You, Lord Jesus.
With all my heart,
I love You, Lord Jesus.
With all my soul,
I love You, Lord Jesus.
With all my mind,
I love You, Lord Jesus.
With all my strength,
I love You, Lord Jesus.
Above all possessions and honors,
I love You, Lord Jesus.
Above all pleasures and enjoyments,
I love You, Lord Jesus.
More than myself and all that belongs to me,
I love You, Lord Jesus.
More than all my relatives and friends,
I love You, Lord Jesus.
More than all persons and all angels,
I love You, Lord Jesus.
Above all created things in Heaven or on earth,
I love You, Lord Jesus.
Only for Yourself,
I love You, Lord Jesus.

A Holy Hour with Mother Angelica

Because You are the Sovereign Good,
I love You, Lord Jesus.
Because You are infinitely worthy of being loved,
I love You, Lord Jesus.
Because You are infinitely perfect,
I love You, Lord Jesus.
Even if You try me by misfortune,
I love You, Lord Jesus.
In wealth and in poverty,
I love You, Lord Jesus.
In prosperity and in adversity,
I love You, Lord Jesus.
In health and in sickness,
I love You, Lord Jesus.
In life and in death,
I love You, Lord Jesus.
In time and in eternity,
I love You, Lord Jesus.
In union with that love, with which the Blessed Virgin
    Mary loves You,
I love You, Lord Jesus.

Let us also pray a Novena prayer to the Holy Spirit:

Father, let Your Spirit come upon us with power to fill us with
His gifts. Make our hearts pleasing to You and ready to do Your
will. We ask this through Our Lord Jesus Christ, who lives
and reigns with You in the unity of the Holy Spirit. Amen.

We have spoken of faith, hope, and love, and we want to ask
the Lord every night before we retire, "Lord, give me an increase
in faith, hope, and love." Because everything we do all day long is

to increase or decrease these three magnificent theological virtues, because they pertain only to God.

I want only one thing for you, and that is for you and all of us here to grow in holiness and love for the Church. And even though you see the Church wounded, you don't make it worse. A wounded Mother deserves your love, your compassion, and the healing power that comes from your prayers and your understanding. So remember: we are here to build, we are not here to destroy. We are here to heal, not to make more wounds. We are here to give. We are here to love. We are here to believe in what the Church teaches — not always to understand but to believe. We saw that so beautifully in how the apostles humbled themselves and obeyed and showed repentant love. We see that so beautifully in the gifts of the Spirit — the gift of hope and the gift of love. You see, there is so much to living the interior life and the spiritual life with the Lord that it is something you must learn every day, every moment. That is what we are here for now. So let's remember together that we're family; let us raise our minds and hearts to God and say, "Lord, we praise You, we bless You, we adore You."

I love you.

Chapter 10

"An Hour of Knowing and Loving Jesus"

Let's talk about knowing Jesus. You can know a lot about Jesus, but never *know* Jesus. How can you do that? You may have a great intellect and memorize Scripture. You may be able to quote chapter and verse of every book in Scripture. So you know a lot *about* God, a lot *about* Jesus, but you may not know Jesus.

You say you want to live a Christian life, so you memorize all those Scripture quotations and you say, "I know Jesus."

Not necessarily.

What does it mean to know Jesus? It means to live with Jesus in your heart — to be aware of His presence to the point, where — this is where we separate the men from the boys — to the point where it affects *the way* you think and *the way* you act. If it doesn't do that, then you know a lot about Him, but you don't know Him. I wonder today if so many of us know a lot *about* Jesus. In fact, a theologian can explain God to you, but he may not really know Jesus in a very personal way.

You, see it does not really take a lot of brains, education, or a high I.Q. It takes a lot of love. When you love much, you experience the Lord. I am not talking about an emotional experience. I mean the kind of experience that makes you want to be like Jesus, so that you are willing to possess and exercise sacrificial love. Sacrificial love which means you're willing to die to yourself and begin to live like Jesus.

A Holy Hour with Mother Angelica

Now, there is a part of Scripture—a very interesting passage—and it says that the disciples had gone to Emmaus. You will find it in Luke 24:13. We are going to find a couple of disciples in this passage—disciples who knew a lot about Jesus but did not know Jesus. You are definitely going to see the difference. When you see this difference, let's examine ourselves and if we do not know Jesus, tell Him, before you go to bed this evening, "Jesus I want to know You. I want my heart to burn with love." Now, these two disciples had heard a lot about the Resurrection, and you can't come down too hard on them, because while they saw Jesus raised from the dead, they were in doubt of it. It was very difficult for them to understand the Divinity of Jesus, which was so far superior to His humanity. In other words, it was the Divinity that raised up His humanity—the Father, the Spirit, the whole Trinity raised His body. And because the disciples could not understand, they were disheartened. So let's not be too hard on them, but it is a great example of how you and I live—maybe most of the time. The Scripture says that "that same day"—that is, the day of the Resurrection—two of them went on their way to a village called Emmaus. Scripture said that they had talked this over. Jesus Himself came up and walked with them, and the amazing thing is that something prevented them from recognizing Jesus. Do you know what that something was? The preoccupation with themselves and their own ideas. If there's one thing to keep us from recognizing Jesus, it's that terrible preoccupation we have with ourselves and our own ideas.

They had an idea that the Lord was a prophet Who was killed, and that was the end of it. It was so strong in their minds—and they felt such self-pity and such distress that all they could think of was their disappointment and that Jesus was not Who or what they thought He was. And they were so immersed in that, they didn't recognize Him.

You and I do that a lot. The tragedy of the present moment is so deep and so horrible sometimes—a child dies, is murdered or killed, or a husband walks out on a wife, and we get so immersed in that moment because it hurts so bad—we don't see Jesus. In the present moment we're doing one thing and something else comes up. We are all immersed in this one thing, we are all interested in it and then something comes up that I've got to leave, and if we don't see Jesus then we are going to get very angry that we are interrupted. Do you see? We don't recognize the Lord. We only recognize the Lord when He looks beautiful and good. But I wonder if we would recognize Him when He was considered a worm and not a man.

So these disciples, you see, did not recognize Him. And what did He say to them? They were walking and He said, "What matters are you discussing as you walk?" And they stopped short. You know what that means—they stopped walking and looked at Him, their faces downcast. Just totally immersed in themselves. They become kind of uppity, and said, "Are you the only one in Jerusalem Who doesn't know the things that have happened?" And Jesus was so loving, and said, "What things?" If there was anybody Who knew what had happened in Jerusalem, it was Jesus! What amazes me about Jesus—well, a lot of things do—He never pounces on us. I would have said, "You stupid disciples, it's Me." I would have poured fire and brimstone on their heads. But Jesus says, "Oh really? Something happened? What happened?" because Jesus is always trying to work from the inside out. He wants it to come from the depths of your heart, not from your head. He wants it to go up. Well, He said, "Tell me all about Jesus." Now listen to what they said. "He proved He was a great prophet," they replied. Oh, there's a big difference between the Messiah, the Son of God, and a prophet. So you see how their hearts were so disheartened and disappointed. They told of how the chief priests and leaders handed Him over to be sentenced to death and had Him crucified. Now comes the real essence of their discouragement: they said, "Our own hope was that He would one day set Israel free." They wanted a political leader. You know, somebody asked me on one of those tours I've been on, "Do you intend to go into politics?" Well I laughed uncontrollably. I reminded them of what the disciples demanded of Jesus — that He deliver them.

From what?

You know, we are so embroiled in social issues today, and not that they don't need to be changed, but our hearts are to the point that we don't want a God who transforms us into holiness, into holy people. We want a God to deliver us from pain, to give us all the food we want, to give us all the help we want; we want a physical Heaven. That's what I mean when I say that we really don't know Jesus. We really don't.

And that is not all the disciples told Jesus. They said that it had been two days and some women (you know, "these emotional women") astounded them and said that they went to the tomb and didn't find the body. The women had said something about how He was alive. Now, you see why they did not recognize Him. They wanted a political leader. They thought He was a prophet; and they were disappointed. In their eyes, these were legitimate reasons not to believe. You wonder sometimes if they really ever knew Jesus. You wonder what they did when Peter said, "Thou art the Christ, the Son of the living God" (see Matthew 16:16). Did they say, "Well, if He is, He will deliver us"? See how our own desires mingle into everything we do, and we spoil it? Well, the Scripture continues, and it says that, "... besides the women, some of our friends" (male friends, I'm sure) "found [the tomb] exactly as the women [had]." It had been Peter and John. And Jesus looked at the disciples and said, "You foolish men. So slow to believe the message."

So, that's the secret of the difference between knowing and believing. The Lord told it to us Himself—we are so slow to believe the full message. That's the difference between knowing about God and knowing God.

Lord God, we, too, are slow of heart. We have our own ideas of Who You are, and what You are, and what You look like, and what You are going to do in our lives, and how to be holy. We have the whole thing planned out, my Lord. We have not really understood the full message of the Cross and of seeing You in the present moment. I ask You to give us all the grace we need to be keenly aware of Your presence and of the real essence of life, and to be transformed into Your image so that we may never lose sight of Who You are and who it is you want us to be. We pray that life will never engulf us to the point that we lose sight of You and Your work, even in the sorrows and sufferings of life. We ask this grace through Jesus Christ, the Messiah Lord. Amen.

Let us pray the Litany to the Holy Name of Jesus:

Jesus, Son of the living God,
have mercy on us.
Jesus, Splendor of the Father,
have mercy on us.
Jesus, Brightness of eternal Light,
have mercy on us.
Jesus, King of Glory,
have mercy on us.
Jesus, Sun of Justice,
have mercy on us.
Jesus, Son of the Virgin Mary,
have mercy on us.

A Holy Hour with Mother Angelica

Jesus, most amiable,
have mercy on us.
Jesus, most admirable,
have mercy on us.
Jesus, the mighty God,
have mercy on us.
Jesus, Father of the world to come,
have mercy on us.
Jesus, angel of great counsel,
have mercy on us.
Jesus, most powerful,
have mercy on us.
Jesus, most patient,
have mercy on us.
Jesus, most obedient,
have mercy on us.
Jesus, meek and humble of heart,
have mercy on us.
Jesus, Lover of Chastity,
have mercy on us.
Jesus, our Lover,
have mercy on us.
Jesus, God of Peace,
have mercy on us.
Jesus, Author of Life,
have mercy on us.
Jesus, Model of Virtues,
have mercy on us.
Jesus, zealous for souls,
have mercy on us.
Jesus, our God,
have mercy on us.

"An Hour of Knowing and Loving Jesus"

Jesus, our Refuge,
have mercy on us.
Jesus, Father of the Poor,
have mercy on us.
Jesus, Treasure of the Faithful,
have mercy on us.
Jesus, good Shepherd,
have mercy on us.
Jesus, true Light,
have mercy on us.
Jesus, eternal Wisdom,
have mercy on us.
Jesus, infinite Goodness,
have mercy on us.
Jesus, our Way and our Life,
have mercy on us.
Jesus, joy of the Angels,
have mercy on us.
Jesus, King of the Patriarchs,
have mercy on us.
Jesus, Master of the Apostles,
have mercy on us.
Jesus, Teacher of the Evangelists,
have mercy on us.
Jesus, Strength of Martyrs,
have mercy on us.
Jesus, Light of Confessors,
have mercy on us.
Jesus, Purity of Virgins,
have mercy on us.
Jesus, Crown of all Saints,
have mercy on us.

A Holy Hour with Mother Angelica

Let us pray. Lord Jesus Christ, You have said, "Ask and you shall receive; seek and you shall find; knock and it shall be opened to you"; mercifully attend to our supplications, and grant us the grace of Your most divine love, that we have love You with all our hearts, and in all our words and actions, and never cease to praise You.

Make us, O Lord, to have a perpetual fear and love of Your holy name, for You never fail to govern those whom You establish in Your love. You, Who live and reign forever and ever. Amen.

You know, the marvelous thing about the disciples going to Emmaus is that they did not recognize the physical presence of Jesus, the man — the God-Man. Isn't it strange and wonderful that they saw Him and only recognized Him in the Eucharist? What a wondrous miracle — the Eucharist, the Real Presence of Jesus. We have to ask ourselves that question: do I recognize the Real Presence of Jesus in the Eucharist as the disciples did? If we can do that, then we will know Jesus.

Holy Michael, the Archangel, defend us in battle. Be our protection against the wickedness and snares of the devil. May God rebuke him, we humbly pray, and do thou, O Prince of the Heavenly Host, by Divine Power thrust into Hell Satan and all the other evil spirits who wander through the world seeking the ruin of souls. Amen.

We ask Our Lord to give us special graces. Not only the gift of knowledge, which will just make us so detached, but also that we will be able to absorb all of God and then let the Lord's love overflow to our neighbor. We also ask for the gift of recognizing Jesus in the Eucharist so that we can look up when the priest holds that beautiful Presence up and say, "My Lord and my God." We have that Presence in the Eucharist, in the chapel all day. We all need to renew our faith. In this world and this time, we must recognize Jesus in our neighbor, in our families and loved ones, and in our fellow workers, in the sufferings of life, and the joys of life. Sometimes we can recognize Him in the sufferings. It's amazing how we then fail to see Jesus in our joys. He gives us both, or at least allows both. So, let us ask the Lord for the gift of knowledge that we may recognize Jesus—especially in the Eucharist.

And when you go out the next time, and you go out into the woods, you can look up into the sky and the trees and at everything that He has created and say again, "My Lord and my God," because He is everywhere. These are little images of His power, of His love, of His greatness, of His omnipotence, of His presence in our midst. So, remember, you are never without His presence—wherever you are, He is there. So, next time you feel kind of lonely, just put your arms around Jesus because He is with you, and He loves you, and love Him in return.

God bless you.

Chapter 11

"An Hour of Prayer"

I bet the disciples used to wonder about prayer, just like you and I wonder about it. Until one day they said, "Master, teach us how to pray" (Luke 11:1). And I think they said it for the same reason that you and I say it. We're just not sure how to talk to God. What do you say to God? We are very good at asking for things. We don't have any problem with asking for things. But we don't always know when we pray. I think people pray a lot more than they realize. Sometimes you say, "Oh, Lord help me." Maybe it's a prayer of desperation, but it's still a prayer. Prayers are often whatever comes from your heart to God expressing your worries, your frustrations, and everything else that happens to you, things that you are not quite sure about.

Some people say, "If You are there — hear me," because our faith is so weak. But you, know that is also a prayer.

The Lord wanted to enlighten the apostles, and He wants to enlighten you and me, and so He describes how to pray to the Father, and then He gives us some very good advice. Some of it I do not think we would ever have thought about, because to us God is so much a God that we don't look upon Him as "Father." But *Abba* means "daddy." I don't know how many people out there call God "daddy," but that's what He wants us to call Him. He wants us to have that totally familiar and filial love for Him. So you can to say anything to Him at any time. He is so much a part of your life that prayer is a Person, not just something that you do. It's Someone you encounter. That's the difference between praying and prayer.

And you know, sometimes some people can make prayer itself their god. When they have the wrong kind of prayer, they become their own god, they become the initiator of all the good things in their life. That is no longer prayer, because that beautiful Someone that we call Jesus is no longer there.

So I want you to look at the eleventh chapter of Luke. In this chapter, the apostles said "Lord, teach us how to pray," and He replies, "When you pray, say, 'Father, may Your name be held holy.'" You know they always called God *Yahweh*, and they trembled when they said the name of God—the great I AM. And so Jesus says not to do that, and to call Him "Father." And He continues, telling us to say, "Thy kingdom come!" And another translation adds, "Your will be done, on earth as it is in Heaven." Then, in the book of Luke, Jesus says to add, "Give us this day our daily bread."

You know, we just do not realize how much of a *now* God is, of how He lives in this present moment and everything is present to Him. He wants you and me to have such total love and such total confidence that we pray for daily bread. It doesn't just mean material bread on your table, but the Eucharist, the Bread of Life—the food—this is the bread. To do the will of God is food for your soul. It builds you into His image.

That's what confused the apostles one day when the Lord said, "I have food that you do not know anything about." They thought, "What kind of food?" Jesus said, "My food is to do the will of the One who sent Me" (John 4:32–34). Do you realize that the accomplishment of the will of God, even if you can't think of anything to say to Him, is the most beautiful prayer you'll ever say in your life?

Why? Because the end of prayer is to make you more and more like Jesus. To absorb the presence of God in a moment when you and He are alone. In the core of your heart, that's where transformation occurs. That is when you are so attuned to God that His Spirit and your spirit become one spirit.

Then Jesus continues: "Forgive us our sins, as we forgive those who sin against us" (see Luke 11:4). Do not forget, when the Lord is saying this, He is talking about prayer. If I forgive a brother who has offended me, I have given to God the most beautiful of prayers. Because whatever the Lord is asking for in the "Our Father" is a part of prayer. Prayers are not just something that I say. They are also something that I do. And to pray well, I must ask for God's grace and help. But I also pray when I accomplish His will and forgive my brother, and also when I ask that God's Kingdom come, and when I pray for poor sinners.

So prayer has both an active and a passive element that you and I cannot forget. Have you ever been so sick that you say, "I can't pray when I'm sick?" Am I to believe that your whole two or three days with flu is lost? Am I to believe that a person who has cancer or some other terminal illness and is in great pain, that before the eyes of God, that is not a prayer? You can't believe that. To suffer and accept the will of God at that moment, even though your poor mind cannot think of one formal prayer or any other kind of prayer, that is still prayer. If you say nothing but "Jesus" and give Him your pain, without question, that is the most beautiful prayer.

So you see, you pray a lot more than you think. And the Lord, knowing us as He does so well, gives us these two examples from Luke 11:5–10. In the first He talks about the man who asks his friend to lend him three loaves of bread. He said, "my friend, lend me three loaves of bread." And the friend says, "Look, don't bother me. My door is bolted." Do you know what that meant? It was not just a question of going down the stairs and opening the door. Everybody had to get up for the father, who was all the way at the end of the room, to unbolt the door. It was a big chore. But the Lord gives us an example. He says, "Don't get discouraged, keep on asking."

And I know some of you have prayed for your children for fifteen or twenty years, just like St. Monica did for St. Augustine. But was her prayer lost? I wonder what would've happened if Monica had stopped praying after fifteen or twenty years. So the Lord says, "Keep on. I want you keep asking Me to the point where you ask, search, and knock relentlessly" (Matthew 7:7). Pray for what you think you need and accept what God gives you. That is a very simple formula for a perfect prayer. Ask for what you need because that's what you think you need.

When I ask for God to give me patience, I'm praying for patience, but you know what I think? I think God thinks I need humility. For if I were more humble, I would be more patient. So, when I pray for patience, I think God says to me, "Sweetheart, what you really need is more humility." My pride comes out in impatience. So I am praying for one thing, but unless I do something about that pride, it's going to come up in some other way. So God gets at the root of things. That's why He says to keep on asking, and never tire.

If you say no to your child and they come back and ask again, you would say "No. Hey, I said no, now that's it." Sometimes we do not ask for good things. That is why our trust level must be so great. I ask for what I think I need, but in my prayer should be the attitude, if not the words, that I will accept whatever God gives me as the very best thing for me.

Lord God, teach us how to pray. Teach us that every sigh that comes from our hearts in times of desperation and anxiety and frustration reaches up to Thee as a cry for help. Teach us that every desire we have, before we are aware of it, You know; that every word we form and speak, You are aware of before we know it. Teach us how to trust. That though we seek and search and knock, let us be so humble of heart that we are confident, trusting and joyful over whatever You give us, knowing You alone know what is best for each one of us. I ask this in the name of Jesus and through the intercession of Mary, His Holy Mother. Amen.

Let us pray the Litany of the Holy Spirit:

Divine Essence, one true God,
have mercy on us.
Spirit of truth and wisdom,
have mercy on us.
Spirit of holiness and justice,
have mercy on us.
Spirit of understanding and counsel,
have mercy on us.
Spirit of love and joy,
have mercy on us.
Spirit of peace and patience,
have mercy on us.
Spirit of longanimity and meekness,
have mercy on us.
Spirit of benignity and goodness,
have mercy on us.
Love substantial of the Father and the Son,
have mercy on us.
Love and life of saintly souls,
have mercy on us.
Fire ever burning,
have mercy on us.

A Holy Hour with Mother Angelica

Living water to quench the thirst of hearts,
have mercy on us.

God, the Holy Spirit, we ask You now to fall afresh upon us,
to melt us, to mold us, to fill us, to use us, to lead us to pray,
to teach us how to pray, to pray in us with groans that go
beyond human ideas, human thoughts and concepts — that
go beyond human words. Holy Spirit, You are the mutual
love that the Father has for Jesus and that Jesus has for the
Father. You, Holy Spirit, the mutual love of the Father and
Jesus, come again and more into our hearts so that our hearts
can be filled with love for one another and for the Father,
for Jesus, and for the unity of You, Holy Spirit, Who are
Love. Thank You, Holy Spirit. Thank You, Jesus. Thank
You, Father. Amen.

Let us pray a Novena prayer to the Holy Spirit:

Father, let Your Spirit come upon us with power to fill us with
His gifts. Make our hearts pleasing to You and ready to do Your
will. We ask this through Our Lord Jesus Christ, who lives
and reigns with You in the unity of the Holy Spirit. Amen.

The gift of counsel is what you need to distinguish between the
human spirit, the Holy Spirit, and the evil spirit. There are many
instances today when you are called upon or encouraged to say different types of prayer that are not of God. And some movements
are not of God. You need to pray every day that the Lord will give
you that intuitive vision, that intuitiveness that says suddenly, "Oh!
This is not of God." That's what the gift of counsel will do for you,
and you need to pray for this gift every day. Those of you who have
been confirmed, ask the Lord every morning, "Lord, renew within
my heart and soul all the gifts that I received at Confirmation," just
like you renew your baptismal vows. I was thrilled recently when

I found out that I was confirmed before I received my First Communion. How it happened, I do not know. But I am most grateful because the Spirit comes in a very special, special way.

Holy Michael, the Archangel, defend us in battle. Be our protection against the wickedness and snares of the devil. May God rebuke him, we humbly pray, and do thou, O Prince of the Heavenly Host, by Divine Power thrust into Hell Satan and all the other evil spirits who wander through the world seeking the ruin of souls. Amen.

We spoke of prayer and the Holy Spirit. We spoke of love. We spoke of dryness in prayer, desolation, the times when you think God has taken a vacation. All of this together, remember, is that little sculpting knife that the Lord uses to cut off all the rough edges that make you and me so unlike Jesus. God is that molder. He transforms. And if you take a lump of clay, you have to work on it before it begins to become something. A sculptor has to chip away, and you almost feel sorry for the marble, how it just flies everywhere! Well, that is what God does to you and me. So remember, do not wait until you feel good to pray. Pray all the time. Just say, "Lord, I love you." Oh, He is so tickled that He just jumps up and down when He hears that, because it means so much for God to hear you say "I love you." You like to hear it. Your husband likes to hear it. Your kids like to hear it. Say it more to everybody. I love you. We need to know that today. And you don't know unless you hear. God wants to hear the greatest prayer of all: "I love you!" The next is, "Thy will be done." It says, "I love You so much, You can do anything You want in my life! I am going to ask for many things — big things. But, if You don't want to give it to me, that's okay. Don't worry about it, Lord. I won't get mad at You." Be simple with God. Pray for parking places and a good cup of tea in a restaurant. You say, "That's what you pray for?" Yes! Don't leave God out of anything in your life. He's just as interested in how a cup of tea tastes to you as He is in your soul. Why? Because He's interested in everything that pleases you. He's interested in everything that happens to you.

Remember to say often, "I love you."

Chapter 12

"On the Feast of the Ascension"

It is Ascension Day! This is the great feast when the Lord ascended into Heaven. Sometimes I've heard people say, "Well, we just don't know too much about the Ascension. I can't really get too excited." I am going to get you very excited because you and I will have an ascension. You say, "We will?" Oh, sure, one day we will. We will rise and shall ascend into the Kingdom, body and soul, at the general resurrection. In Matthew 28:16–17, the very last paragraph, it says, "Meanwhile, the eleven disciples went into Galilee, to the mountain Jesus had directed them to go. When they saw Him, they worshipped Him; but some doubted." Isn't that amazing? You know the Lord had been with the apostles for almost forty days, and still they hesitated.

What does it take for some people to believe? *What does it take?* Were they still disappointed that He did not deliver them from Rome? Did they still want a political leader? Were they still not sure? Maybe they weren't sure what was happening. Maybe they thought, "What's going to happen?" But you would think they would just throw themselves on the ground and say, "Oh, my Lord and my God," like St. Thomas did. Yet, some hesitated.

"And Jesus drew near and spoke to them saying, 'All power in Heaven and on earth has been given to Me'" (Matthew 28:18). You've got to listen to this: *"All power in Heaven and on earth has been given to Me.*" So Jesus has total authority over Heaven and earth and under the earth. He then said, "Go therefore."

And why did Jesus want to say He had this authority? As a Catholic, I feel very consoled by this. Why? Because Jesus gave that authority to Peter and all that followed after Peter. And the reason He wanted them to know that He had authority on earth was because He wanted to give that authority to others. Then He said, "Go and preach." So someone—the Son of God—had authority to tell Peter and all those that followed after Peter they could go and make disciples of all nations, and baptize them in the name of the Father and the Son and the Holy Spirit. And what else did Jesus say? "Teach them to observe all the commands I gave you" (Matthew 28:20).

There are three things He told them to do. He said they were, first, to make disciples (that is, those who follow Jesus); second, that they were to baptize; and third, that they were to teach.

You know, today we have an awful lot of people doing two of these but not the first. We have a lot of people baptizing and we have an awful lot of people teaching to observe the commandments. But the first one is first for a reason. That's because when you are a disciple, you are committed. You begin to think like Jesus and act like Jesus. Religion becomes kind of a person to you. It's not something that you do, it is not something you observe. When you are a good citizen you observe the law, but you do not become the law. But when you are a committed disciple, you become like the One you follow. There's a great difference. And Our Lord, knowing how hard it would be, said, "Behold I am with you all days, even unto the consummation of the world" (Matthew 28:20). There is never a moment He is not with us. As a Catholic, I just do not know what I would do without the Eucharist. I seriously do not know what I would do.

Someone came to me yesterday and wanted to know how I get rid of my frustrations. I said, "I don't have that much frustration." They said "You must have a tremendous amount of frustration." I said, "Well I do get frustrated." There is no question of that. I get angry and sometimes I get impatient. I just go before the Blessed Sacrament and I just sit there. And I don't even tell the Lord what's wrong. He knows. Sometimes I babble because I am angry. Then, suddenly, you know, I get the light to say, "Angelica, that is foolish."

"Trust me," Our Lord says. "I know what I am doing." I have to ascend.

You see, we ignore this little paragraph sometimes, because we say, "Well, the Lord went up. So now what?" What you do not understand is that He brought everybody to Heaven. Can you imagine the time that Adam and Eve and all these prophets first saw the Kingdom and the light of glory — the Father — face-to-face? Can you imagine all of the disciples that were to come would only go to Heaven because Jesus went there first and opened the door?

Oh, I know what some of you are thinking. "Oh, now, wait a minute, Mother. Jesus promised Paradise to the thief. He did not go to Heaven, but to Paradise, which we call Limbo." Well, no one went to Heaven until Jesus took them there. They were the fruit of His suffering, His redemption — the first fruits — and you and I are that same fruit. We have the same commission from God as you read in John: "You have not chosen Me, but I have chosen you and have appointed you that you should go and bear fruit, and that your fruit should remain" (John 15:16).

He says here to make disciples. You don't know how to make disciples? You say, "How do I make disciples?" Well, you know, there's a fantastic thing that happens through examples. You know why some of your children are what they are: because of bad examples. Television gives bad examples, newspapers and magazines, billboards and ads. It is like a magnetic tool. Bad examples pull and we are inclined to evil, much more easily than to virtue. We're dragged into evil things or bad things or less than good things because our fallen nature tends in that direction.

But Jesus is saying that His grace is so powerful, His presence is so powerful. And that is why He says this about the Eucharist: "Unless you eat My Flesh and drink My Blood you shall not have life in you" (John 6:53). I need to have God Himself inside of me to become like Him. I cannot forgive unless Jesus is within me to forgive. I cannot persevere in trial, in pain, in heartache, and in frustration if I do not have God's grace within me. I cannot do a thing, not one thing.

And so you see this other example of your total dependence upon the Lord and being able to be serene and joy-filled. Not happy; happiness is for the next life — but joy-filled, which, in this life, enables you and me to withstand and persevere in our faith and hope and love through pain, tragedy, heartache and disappointment.

So, when Jesus ascended, He gave us a vision of what's to come. And you need to keep that vision in your mind. Don't think of Heaven. You know when my grandfather was very sick, we did not dare invite the priest in to give him the last rites. Why? Because he got into a frenzy, thinking, "I'm gonna die, I'm gonna die." A typical Italian reaction. No one told him it was the preparation to see the Heavens open and all those glorious saints, and most of all to see the Holy Trinity — to be able to see them face-to-face.

And that's what Jesus did, this glorious day. We've got to look deeper than even this little bit of Scripture to understand it. It is our hope! It is what makes this life, with all its problems, worthwhile. And, one day, you and I shall be there in Heaven with all those wonderful men and women who have gone ahead of us, given us examples and paved the way for you and me to be transformed. That is our goal. We just don't want to be good. We just don't want to be holy. We want to be transformed into the image of Jesus so that we see with the eyes of God.

And so I hope you ascend. I hope that in your memory and your intellect and your will, you will ascend above all your problems—at least for today.

Lord God, give us all the grace we need to ascend above ourselves, above the things around us, that we may never lose sight of Thy Kingdom, of Thy awesome presence, Thy presence within us, Thy presence around us, Thy presence above us, Thy presence beneath us. We pray that we hold firm the belief that everywhere we go and in everything we do, You are present to give us courage and strength and hope. So let our hearts and our minds ascend often above the things of this world, that we may live now as we shall one day live in Thy Kingdom. Amen.

Let us pray the Litany of the Holy Name of Jesus:

Jesus, Son of the living God,
have mercy on us.
Jesus, Splendor of the Father,
have mercy on us.
Jesus, Brightness of eternal Light,
have mercy on us.
Jesus, King of Glory,
have mercy on us.
Jesus, Sun of Justice,
have mercy on us.
Jesus, Son of the Virgin Mary,
have mercy on us.
Jesus, most amiable,
have mercy on us.
Jesus, most admirable,
have mercy on us.

A Holy Hour with Mother Angelica

Jesus, the mighty God,
have mercy on us.
Jesus, Father of the world to come,
have mercy on us.
Jesus, angel of great counsel,
have mercy on us.
Jesus, most powerful,
have mercy on us.
Jesus, most patient,
have mercy on us.
Jesus, most obedient,
have mercy on us.
Jesus, meek and humble of heart,
have mercy on us.
Jesus, Lover of Chastity,
have mercy on us.
Jesus, our Lover,
have mercy on us.
Jesus, God of Peace,
have mercy on us.
Jesus, Author of Life,
have mercy on us.
Jesus, Model of Virtues,
have mercy on us.
Jesus, zealous for souls,
have mercy on us.
Jesus, our God,
have mercy on us.
Jesus, our Refuge,
have mercy on us.
Jesus, Father of the Poor,
have mercy on us.

Jesus, Treasure of the Faithful,
have mercy on us.
Jesus, good Shepherd,
have mercy on us.
Jesus, true Light,
have mercy on us.
Jesus, eternal Wisdom,
have mercy on us.
Jesus, infinite Goodness,
have mercy on us.
Jesus, our Way and our Life,
have mercy on us.
Jesus, joy of the Angels,
have mercy on us.
Jesus, King of the Patriarchs,
have mercy on us.
Jesus, Master of the Apostles,
have mercy on us.
Jesus, Teacher of the Evangelists,
have mercy on us.
Jesus, Strength of Martyrs,
have mercy on us.
Jesus, Light of Confessors,
have mercy on us.
Jesus, Purity of Virgins,
have mercy on us.
Jesus, Crown of all Saints,
have mercy on us.

Let us pray. Lord Jesus Christ, You have said, "Ask and you
shall receive; seek and you shall find; knock and it shall be
opened to you"; mercifully attend to our supplications, and

grant us the grace of Your most divine love, that we have love You with all our hearts, and in all our words and actions, and never cease to praise You.

Make us, O Lord, to have a perpetual fear and love of Your holy name, for You never fail to govern those whom You establish in Your love. You, Who live and reign forever and ever. Amen.

Let us pray a Novena prayer to the Holy Spirit:

Father, let Your Spirit come upon us with power to fill us with His gifts. Make our hearts pleasing to You and ready to do Your will. We ask this through Our Lord Jesus Christ, who lives and reigns with You in the unity of the Holy Spirit. Amen.

We want to pray always for fortitude in everything, and for perseverance as well, because sometimes you let your defenses down and, all of a sudden, things just go wrong on every side. In order to pray for perseverance, in order to protect ourselves, once again, we pray this prayer to St. Michael the Archangel:

Holy Michael, the Archangel, defend us in battle. Be our protection against the wickedness and snares of the devil. May God rebuke him, we humbly pray, and do thou, O Prince of the Heavenly Host, by the Divine Power thrust into Hell Satan and all the other evil spirits who wander through the world seeking the ruin of souls. Amen.

We ask the Lord to bless us every morning, and any time you see a priest, ask him for his blessing. It is so important. We all perhaps envy the apostles and the children who used to sit on Our Lord's knees and get His blessing. The blessing of a priest is the blessing of Jesus! And it does not matter if you like your priest or do not like him. Maybe he doesn't give the sermons that you like. It doesn't matter. The fact that he is an ordained priest of God makes his blessing extremely powerful. So, whenever you meet a priest, say, "Father, give me your blessing." Why? Because the Spirit of the Lord fills you.

When we talk about fortitude and counsel and all those marvelous gifts of the Spirit that enable us to be holy as God is holy, and compassionate and merciful as He is compassionate and merciful, we need all the help we can get. Our Lady has asked us over and over to pray often for the Holy Spirit. Pray to the Holy Spirit, pray for His gifts. It is through the Holy Spirit that the Precious Blood of Jesus falls upon you and that you receive all these marvelous sacraments—that you are forgiven, that you receive the Eucharist, Baptism, and all the rest. So, Holy Spirit, come and live in our hearts.

Chapter 13

"An Hour of the Beatitudes — The First Three"

Something that is extremely important is a kind of spiritual blueprint, and a spiritual blueprint is the Beatitudes. Jesus was very specific as to how to attain holiness of life. We can never say, "I have no idea how to be holy," because Jesus gave us the parables and they were very simple. And the Beatitudes are in the book of Matthew, chapter five. Let's look there now.

When you read Scripture, use another faculty you have — your imagination. Most people just read and dump it into their memory, and kind of intellectualize what they read, but I think if you use your imagination as well, it puts a little spirit into it.

Scripture says, "Seeing the crowds, He went up the hill." I want you to imagine, right now, a hill. It isn't obviously very big, but Jesus walked up a hill, and once there, He sat down, perhaps on a large rock looking out over the crowd. Then He began to speak. Of course, that's what the crowd went there for. I can imagine Our Lord just being a magnificent speaker with a very manly low voice — very powerful, enunciating every word and making it so perfect, but in such a way that it did not make you uncomfortable. It made it so that it absorbed into your heart, so that it was not merely words like other men gave, sermons of doctors of the law. It seemed to be a penetrating Word. A Word that got into your mind and then rested in your heart. They were mesmerized as soon as He sat down.

A Holy Hour with Mother Angelica

So, they knew it was coming and they would look at Him and wait for that special Word. And this particular day, He said something that needed a lot of thought. And they would take the word of the rabbi or the word of Jesus in this case and they would ponder it. In fact, it says Our Lady pondered these words. That means they kind of mulled it over in their minds. "I wonder what He meant by this," they would think; "What *does this* mean?" And then they would talk to each other about it. They did not have the distraction of TV or radio and all the rest. They talked about the Law and the about the Scriptures, and they found tremendous fulfillment.

You and I have lost the art of speaking to God. See, that is an art. If speech comes just from the heart, it's not entirely there. When it comes from the heart and from the mind together, then it's an art. Because it gives and receives. If a sermon is one-sided, then there's something wrong with it. It has to give and receive.

So we see in the First Beatitude. The Lord said, "Blessed are the poor in spirit, for theirs is the Kingdom of Heaven" (see Matthew 5:3). What does that mean? Does it mean the poor? Does it mean those who have nothing of this world's goods? No, because some of the poor are rich in the heart, and some are bitter, angry, resentful. Jesus says that it is the "poor in spirit," so it cannot mean the physical things that you do not have. What does it mean? And is it strange that the Lord says "in spirit"? I think He knew that many of us can be without possessions and not really be poor. To be "poor in spirit" means a lot of things. Did you ever go through a dry spell? Did you ever go through a spell where you want to pray, you thirst for God, but nothing comes to your mind and nothing comes to your heart? And suddenly, you just don't know what to do. You think God has taken a trip, a vacation. Aren't you then poor in spirit? What does it mean? It means that you have nothing of yourself to depend upon. Your memory does not work; you cannot imagine anything; you can't think of anything; and you just don't particularly even want to pray. So all of the faculties that the Lord has given you seem to be dulled. So if you are poor in spirit, you just go to prayer during that hard time. Why? Because you have nothing but your misery to give to God. The poor have a tremendous amount of misery.

I was poor the whole time when I was a kid. Misery was my position, thought I had it forever, it was all I expected to have. But when I can attribute this feeling to my soul and not to physical things, when my soul has nothing but its own misery, then I begin to understand I am proud and sometimes arrogant and sometimes impatient and sometimes sensitive. Then I am willing to stand before the Lord in all my misery and say, "Lord I give You the only things that are mine: my sins and my will. I have nothing else."

To be able to sit in the chapel or sit in your living room and feel your memory, but to have your mind and heart rest with the glory of the Lord. In other words, to get to a point where we can totally forget our misery, though we feel it and are sore. And that's where the Lord says here, "The Kingdom of Heaven is yours." And we don't relate union with God with misery. We relate it to ecstasy and good feelings and consolations. And we demand those things from God. In fact, that's our criteria for His pleasure and His good will towards us, so we are constantly lamenting. Someone may ask, "How are you with the Lord?" "Miserable," you say. Praise God! Why? Because the Kingdom of Heaven is yours, there is nothing of yourself that is of any value anymore. You really see yourself as you are.

Today's world is really smothering spirituality out of you, because it has positive thinkers. I mean those people who think that no matter how rotten you are, you feel good, good, good; and you are getting better, better, better. We have taken the beauty of God's spirituality and turned it around into nothing. You say, "Well isn't that what you are talking about, being nothing before the Lord?" No. I am talking about being yourself before the Lord. And being willing, being content. To me, to be poor in spirit is to be content with God alone. To say to God, "Lord, I give you everything."

Do you remember when the Lord said to Peter, "Do you love Me more than these?" (John 21:15). We say, "Well, He's talking about the apostles, maybe." But I think He also meant these other worldly things. Because Peter said, "What about this man?" later on, meaning St. John. And the Lord said, "Don't worry about him." So Peter had a lot of things on his mind. And the Lord said to Peter, "Do you love Me more than these things?"

This morning, I got up and tried it. The first thing that hit my mind was some problem with the network. I said, "No, Lord, I love You more than these things." Then I said, "I am just going to drop the whole thing into Your lap. I am going to look at You face-to-face today. You take care of it! I love You more than these. I love You more than myself. I love You more than my feelings, my desire for feeling. I love You more than my desire to know where I am and how I am doing. I love You more than anything or anyone. So, I look at You and let the rest fall away.

That's poverty of spirit. You say, "Mother, are you saying I shouldn't worry about things?" Well, I think we can be concerned. But we should never worry to the point that they attract our love and attention and take them away from the Lord. Especially during prayer time. You have a lot of time during the day, and it's a strange phenomenon. If you have spent your day with the Lord and a crisis comes along, you will handle it. If an opportunity comes along to make a decision, you'll see the light. Why? Because you have been with the Lord and the light is bright. You know it's hard to discern when you're on one of these levels and full of self.

And so being "poor in spirit" is to abandon yourself to the will of God. It is to be so empty of ourselves that we prefer

Jesus. I have a preferential love, which means I prefer Him to all things. I am willing to feel my miserable condition, to admit my faults, sins and weaknesses, and to lift my eyes to God and say, "How great Thou art." It means I would give up mother, father, brother, sister, friends, and possessions for His sake. We always relate that to a vocation to the religious life. But I think He said it for everybody. It didn't mean you're supposed to leave everything and everyone; that's not life. God doesn't ask you to do anything impossible.

I think it is meant that we are not to be possessed by the world, by the flesh, by the enemy. To be totally free. That's what this Beatitude means. That is why the Lord put it first. We are to be totally free. We are to trust to the level where I know my God loves me and He will take care of everything. When I reach that level, I am truly poor in spirit.

> Lord God, I praise You and bless You. I thank You for the light to see my faults and weaknesses and my imperfections and my sins. Give me the grace to look up at Thee and say, "Lord, how pure and holy and great Thou art. When I feel dry and feel like You have taken a vacation, Lord, let me sit in the silence of my room and listen to Your awesome presence. Let me be content with my lot in the miseries of today, knowing that Your providence rises before the dawn. Let me be poor in spirit that the Kingdom of Heaven may be my only possession. Amen."

The next two Beatitudes Jesus gave us are:

Blessed are the meek, for they shall possess the earth.
Blessed are they who mourn, for they shall be comforted.

To mourn and to be meek and gentle of heart does not mean you are a doormat or a rug. It does not mean that you just take it from everybody. Jesus certainly did not, and He was the meekest of the meek, a Lamb getting ready for the slaughter.

As you pray these Beatitudes, remember, it's okay to be dry in spirit, not to feel like praying, to feel like you have not made any progress. We need to know that God is not looking at the veneer that everybody else looks at. And it has become something that we concentrate on so much, because we feel our miseries. Go into the core of your hearts, into the very center of your heart. Be content that you are not perfect. It does not mean that you do not strive to be better, and certainly you never fall into mortal sin. But it means that there are certain parts of your mind and being that are imperfect. I have been striving for patience for years. I have been a nun for forty-three years and sometimes I think, "Oh, Angelica, you have kind of made it!" And *whoosh*, down the tube. And it's always going to be that way. And, sometimes it takes a little bit longer. Maybe it's four or five days now that I don't blow my stack, but all of a sudden, just when I think I've made it, the Lord says "Angelica, you have a little bit to go yet." And that's a good sign. It means that I know exactly how unlike Jesus I am, and I can strive to be better.

Let us pray the Litany of Divine Providence:

God All-knowing and All-wise,
have mercy on us.
God All-powerful and All-good,
have mercy on us.
God most patient and most merciful,
have mercy on us.
God of Mercy and Consolation,
have mercy on us.
God, wonderful and inscrutable in Your plan,
have mercy on us.

"An Hour of the Beatitudes — The First Three"

God in Whose hands is our life,

have mercy on us.

God from Whom all good things and every perfect gift
comes,

have mercy on us.

God Who has made all things for our service,

have mercy on us.

God Who governs all with wisdom and love,

have mercy on us.

You Who fill all living things with blessing,

have mercy on us.

You Who do clothe the lilies of the field and feed the
birds of the air,

have mercy on us.

You Who number the hairs of our heads,

have mercy on us.

You Who sees in secret,

have mercy on us.

You Who makes the sun to shine upon the good and the
bad,

have mercy on us.

You Who allows it to rain upon the just and the unjust,

have mercy on us.

You Who work all things for the benefit of those who love
You,

have mercy on us.

You Who send temporal sufferings for correction and for
our own good,

have mercy on us.

You who reward Christian patience with an eternal
reward,

have mercy on us.

A Holy Hour with Mother Angelica

God, our only refuge and our only hope,
have mercy on us.
God, Our Only Consoler and Our Only Helper,
have mercy on us.

God, Our Father, we come to You in and with and through Jesus Christ, Your Only Son. You have sent us a Savior and Our Only Mediator. We trust in You. We trust in Your plan... Help us, Father, to follow Your Son, Jesus; to follow Your plan with poverty of spirit; when mourning and looking for the comfort that You give, to follow Your plan with meekness. Thank You, Father. We ask this through Jesus Christ, Your Son, who lives and reigns with You in the unity of the Holy Spirit, One God, forever and ever. Amen.

When we pray the Beatitudes and ask the Lord for grace, I think sometimes we need to know that the enemy does everything possible to keep us from persevering in these Blessed Beatitudes.

Holy Michael the Archangel, defend us in battle. Be our protection against the wickedness and snares of the devil. May God rebuke him, we humbly pray, and do thou, O Prince of the Heavenly Host, by Divine Power thrust into Hell Satan and all other evil spirits who wander through the world seeking the ruin of souls. Amen.

We need to pray to the holy angels that they may assist us in our journey home and in the acquisition and growth of these fantastic Beatitudes.

You know you ought to make a little Sign of the Cross on your foreheads. Husbands on your wives' foreheads, and wives on your husbands' foreheads, and on your children's foreheads before they go to school. Just make a little cross. There's a power in the Cross, and when a priest blesses you in the Sign of the Cross, it is tremendous.

Make the Sign of the Cross often during the day. When you feel a temptation around you, make the Sign of the Cross, because in the Sign of the Cross the demons are in terror. In the Sign of the Cross is your strength. In the Sign of the Cross is your hope. In the Sign of the Cross is that beautiful strength and grace that makes you contented — that you can be poor in spirit, that you can mourn, and that you can be meek and humble of heart. This is our heritage. We are not a violent people, though, at times, we are angry. We are not a depressed people, there are times we are most joyful. We are a people in the Lord ready to be blessed because we seek His will.

Chapter 14

"An Hour of the Beatitudes—The Next Three"

Today we're reading St. Matthew's Gospel 5:6.

One of the Beatitudes that I think is extremely important is the one that states, "Blessed are they who hunger and thirst for justice, for they shall be satisfied."

And I wonder if it's exercised today, and in what way is it exercised. So the Lord is saying that you should seek holiness, goodness, righteousness. If you seek those, then you hunger and thirst. You know, there is a great difference between hunger and thirst. You can do without food for quite a long time, but you cannot do without water. In the spiritual life, you can't go very long without hunger and thirst for God. In the life of the body, we alleviate this hunger and thirst as soon as possible. We eat three times a day, or at least once a day, and we drink a lot. Health experts recommend at least eight glasses of water a day.

So, in the sense of the body, you have to satisfy hunger and thirst. The Lord is saying that. He said, "You shall be satisfied." Yet we know that sometimes the spiritual life is just the opposite of the physical life. In the physical life, I feed my body and whatever I fed it yesterday is gone today. But in the spiritual life, I must hunger for God and I must continue hungering for God, I must continue to thirst for God, too. Without that, there is no zeal—and there is nothing that keeps prodding me in the midst of pain and sorrow and dryness.

A Holy Hour with Mother Angelica

Perseverance is the fruit of hungering and thirsting for God. I cannot persevere in holiness of life—my body rebels, the world rebels, the flesh rebels, the enemy rebels so I have rebellion all around me when I say I seek holiness—unless I have a deep hunger, and the hunger is fed by the Eucharist. That is our source of constant grace. So is reading the Scripture, so is performing acts of love and charity. But there is a difference. I can do a beautiful act of love for someone, make them a pie or lead them across the street, and still not have the right motivation. I may want to be seen by men. I can fast to appear holy. That, of course, is what the Pharisees did. I can say loud prayers on the street corners. I can't see hunger for God, because nobody ever sees that. Everything we do for the body, everybody sees. But when I hunger and thirst for God, it is something so deep inside of me that I cannot share it with my brother. I could say I had a dry day and did not feel like praying. But nobody knows the pain of that statement—*the pain*. Have you ever missed somebody? Think of the person you love the most and suddenly that person takes off and goes three or four states away, goes to school, goes to live someplace else. And there is such a desire that we call hunger, a desire to see them, to speak to them, to be with them. What is it? Where do you hurt if you miss someone? In your heart. You don't get a headache. It's in your heart. You hunger to be with that person. So, we have to have the same hunger for God. And we start with repentance.

First of all, I must know my sins. Today, though, we are told to ignore them, and it's called self-fulfillment. If someone says this or that is a sin, they are said to lack compassion or that they are rashly judging you. (You know, what we need today is a good John the Baptist type of person who says, "Repent, repent of your sins and have a transformation of life!")

If you hunger for God, some of you are in deep sin. You have a desire for God, and you want to get out of that sin in the worst way.

But you need repentance. You need to say, "O God, I am so sorry." That's why the Beatitude of "Blessed are those who mourn" is ahead of it because you must mourn sins. I must say, "God, I have sinned against You and Heaven, and I am sorry." Then the floodgates of mercy open up and you begin to hunger for God.

And what about thirst? What does it mean to thirst for God? It means you have God and you want more and more and more. Hunger is the beginning, the foundation of which is repentance. The foundation of thirst is humility. I must never forget who I am and what I am capable of. I must never forget I was a sinner, I am a sinner, and that it is only God's mercy that I must depend upon.

So, hunger is that change of life when I get that vacuum inside of me that says there has got to be something else. There's got to be more. So we begin with hunger, and soon, as I begin to see God and know God and begin to be filled with God, I want more and more and more. And that's thirst. You have to have both. It isn't that you're hungry and then it passes, because as Scripture says, the just man, the holy man, falls seven times a day. We are always in that process of seeking healing and forgiveness. Every night we need to be healed. We need to be repentant. We need to be forgiven.

When you have that kind of concept and reality in your heart, fed by the Eucharist, the Body and Blood, Soul and Divinity of Jesus, the thirst for God, you get a peace that comes down upon you and within you. What is a sense of peace? A sense that you know there is a God. He knows you. He loves you. And He is within you. You know that little truth. And you're going to want more of God.

So, we are going to thirst for God with a thirst for Him until we die. And that thirst is a pain, and that hunger is a pain, just like in the physical life. But it's a good pain. It's a healthy sign. Everybody says, "I want to be sure I love God. I want a sign that I love God." Do you hunger and thirst? You say, "Well, I hunger and thirst, but I am not getting anywhere." Oh, but that's part of hungering and thirsting! What is it that makes you want God more and more if it isn't the reality that you're such a bum? Oh, society says, "I'm not a bum. I mean, I've got it all together." No, you don't. You've fallen apart. Say it's so. "I am falling apart. Lord God, put me together." We want truth, we don't want to hide under some kind of psychoanalysis. I'm not going to hide under so-called positive thinking. You have sinned and you are a sinner. Repent. "You sound like a 'Hell and Brimstone' minister," you say. I don't care what I sound like. I'm not here to win friends and influence people. I want to tell you the truth. If you don't hunger and thirst for God, you can never be satisfied. It says here, all you people boozing it up, sexing it up, running after honor and glory and money and cars and boats, you are never to be satisfied. Because you're gone, you're putting everything down a limitless hole. There is no end to the desires man has for this world. You are only hindered by your own finite capacity. But with God, hunger and thirst can be satisfied because only with God and prayer, the Eucharist and Mary — to pray with us and pray for us, put her protective mantle around us — can we ever hope to have the holy hunger and holy thirst it takes to make us go on, no matter how we feel, no matter how tired we are, no matter how dry we are, no matter how many obstacles are in our way. We doggedly go forward.

And that brings us to the fifth Beatitude.

Blessed are the merciful, for they shall obtain mercy.

Let's ask God for this great Beatitude.

Lord God, I am a sinner. I ask for mercy, for it is only in Your mercy, Lord, that I am free. Give me this Beatitude, give me the grace to hunger for the higher gifts, to be detached from this transitory world where everything passes so quickly. When I have found You, let me hold on to You; let me thirst for more and more grace and holiness and to love You in prayer—that I may arrive at that holiness You have designed for me before I was born, before I was conceived. I ask You, Lord, I ask for Your forgiveness. I ask for Your mercy. Amen.

Let us pray the Litany of the Most Precious Blood of Jesus:

Blood of Christ, only-begotten Son of the Eternal Father,

save us.

Blood of Christ, Incarnate Word of God,

save us.

Blood of Christ, of the New and Eternal Testament,

save us.

Blood of Christ, falling upon the earth in the Agony,

save us.

Blood of Christ, shed profusely in the Scourging,

save us.

Blood of Christ, flowing forth in the Crowning with Thorns,

save us.

Blood of Christ, poured out on the Cross,

save us.

Blood of Christ, price of our salvation,

save us.

Blood of Christ, without which there is no forgiveness.

save us.

Blood of Christ, Eucharistic drink and refreshment of souls,

save us.

A Holy Hour with Mother Angelica

Blood of Christ, stream of mercy,
save us.
Blood of Christ, victor over demons,
save us.
Blood of Christ, courage of Martyrs,
save us.
Blood of Christ, strength of Confessors,
save us.
Blood of Christ, bringing forth Virgins,
save us.
Blood of Christ, help of those in peril,
save us.
Blood of Christ, relief of the burdened,
save us.
Blood of Christ, solace in sorrow,
save us.
Blood of Christ, hope of the penitent,
save us.
Blood of Christ, consolation of the dying,
save us.
Blood of Christ, peace and tenderness of hearts,
save us.
Blood of Christ, pledge of eternal life,
save us.
Blood of Christ, freeing souls from purgatory,
save us.
Blood of Christ, most worthy of all glory and honor,
save us.

Let us pray. Almighty and eternal God, You have appointed
Your only-begotten Son the Redeemer of the world, and
willed to be appeased by His Blood. Grant we beg of You,

that we may worthily adore this price of our salvation, and through its power be safeguarded from the evils of the present life, so that we may rejoice in its fruits forever in Heaven. Through the same Christ our Lord. Amen.

You know, if you notice these Beatitudes, they follow in the right order because if we hunger and thirst for what is right, the fruit of that is mercy. We are going to be merciful. Why? Because I am so aware of my sinful condition. If I am aware of this condition, how can I find fault with you? If I am aware of the two-by-four beam in my eye, how am I going to look at the splinter in your eye? So, I am going to be merciful to you. And if I am merciful, I have got to be pure of heart. You say, "Well how does that follow?" Because we're not pure of heart when we continually find fault with other people. If we could say honestly say we had seen or found the worst sinner in the world—or the one who seems to be a sinner, anyway—we would be the same way if not for the grace of God. I would be in the same position if I had the opportunity. Most of us are not big sinners because we lack opportunity—not ability, but opportunity. That's the point. And so, if you were thrown into opportunities like our kids are today—all over the streets they have to sell their bodies to eat, for example—are you sure you wouldn't do the same? So we cannot judge and we cannot be unmerciful. We need to be merciful. So if I am going to be merciful to my neighbor, I am going to have a pure heart. What makes my heart impure? We always equate purity with sex. We have what I call "sexitis" in society today. But purity of heart means I want God. I want to be like God. I want to imitate God.

And, so all of these Beatitudes follow until you reach the essence. If you were to take the seven gifts of the Holy Spirit, they would match the Beatitudes. It's an amazing phenomenon. You ought to do it sometime—it's what I call Scripture fun. Do you ever have Scripture fun? You ought to try it. One kind of Scripture fun is to compare what Jesus said in one place with another place. It is really amazing how the whole blueprint of the spiritual life is in the Beatitudes and the seven gifts of the Holy Spirit given in Isaiah, chapter 11, and then matched those with the seven petitions in the Our Father prayer. They all say basically the same thing. They all lead to the ultimate holiness in this life, which we call transforming union, as St. Paul writes in Corinthians, until we are turned into the image we reflect. So we reflect Jesus as we really put these Beatitudes into practice. Some of them, we say, "Oh, aren't they nice? Don't they sound pretty?" But you've got to live them. They don't always sound nice. They are very difficult — just like everything God told us to do is very difficult. But we have spiritual positive thinkers, who make you think it's just joy, joy, joy all the time when in fact it's actually difficult. If your gospel isn't hard, I don't know whose gospel you have.

And we need to pray very hard sometimes for protection. My sisters and I pray for protection every day from every kind of evil.

Holy Michael the Archangel, defend us in battle. Be our protection against the wickedness and snares of the devil. May God rebuke him, we humbly pray, and do thou, O Prince of the Heavenly Host, by Divine Power thrust into Hell Satan and all the other evil spirits who wander through the world seeking the ruin of souls. Amen.

Let us this week not live in darkness; there is so much darkness. Be a light on top of a mountain. Take the bushel basket off your light and let it shine. It is not against humility to let your light shine. Why? Because the Lord said it should shine. You are the salt of the earth, an example of holiness and desire for Jesus and the joy of Jesus in the midst of pain; the peace of Jesus in the midst of turmoil; the perseverance of Jesus through every obstacle because

He had one thing in mind: you. He was driven by His love for you. Are you driven by His love for you? Are you driven by your love for Him? Sometimes, we are driven by many things, but not because we love Jesus.

So, let's just make a resolution to spend a few moments in quiet prayer before Jesus, before you just buzz around the house again, and ask Jesus to give you the grace to be so in love with Him that it is that love that drives you to holiness.

Chapter 15

"An Hour of the Beatitudes—The Final Three"

The Beatitudes follow each other, and every single Beatitude leads us to another avenue in the spiritual life that brings us closer and closer to the Lord. It is like a degree of prayer, a degree of holiness, a degree of self-giving, a degree of emptying oneself until you get to the very last. It is very attuned to the seven gifts of the Holy Spirit.

In Matthew 5:9, it says, "Blessed are the peacemakers, for they shall be called sons of God."

In today's world, we look upon a peacemaker as someone who makes peace between warring nations, feuding families, disgruntled friends, and troubled marriages. So too, the peace that we make is always dealing with an absence of something—an absence of love; an absence of peace meaning serenity; an absence of conformity. So it's always an absence when we talk about worldly peace. The peace that the Lord is talking about focuses on a presence. It is just the opposite, but higher than worldly peace. For example, peace is an absence of war. Peace in the world is an absence of turmoil. You have to talk to a person and ask, "How are you?" They might reply, "I feel very peaceful today." And you may ask, "Why do you feel peaceful?" They could respond, "Everything is going well." So it is an absence of their cross; an absence of suffering; an absence of pain. Always an absence. No matter what you do when you talk about peace in the world, it's an absence. In a country, peace means that somewhere along the line we must make people happy with each other so that we may have peace.

But in the spiritual life, the way we talk about opposites, because we are dealing with two different Kingdoms, we speak about a presence. It is by making peace with that presence that we acquire serenity. That's how I am a child of God. St. Peter says that we are adopted sons of God, meaning that His presence is in me. It is not as if He writes me a letter and says "I adopt you." He is flesh of my flesh and bone of my bone because He lives in me through the power of Baptism.

Well, how do I make peace with God? That's the important thing. If I have left the Lord—if I have seriously, grievously, sinned against Him—I need to make peace with Him. How do I do that? Through Reconciliation. One of the almost lost sacraments today. It bothers me—I heard a priest say that everybody goes to Communion and very few go to Confession. This priest told me that he sits in the confessional and nobody comes. A few old people come, maybe.

Are we making peace with God? How am I going to be a child of God if I don't have Him living within me? If I throw Him out by sin, by grievous sin, then I am not a child of God any longer. At that point, I am living in turmoil. I live in Hell. You know, some of you think that sin is lots of fun. One of the saddest news commentaries I have heard in a long, long time, was when a teenager being interviewed said she was so happy for condoms because now she can have fun on a date. I thought what a horrible—horrible—way to live. Does she really know what she is saying? That fun to her is alienation from God. If any of you are alienated from God by sin, let me tell you, you are going to have *short-lived* fun and *long* misery. Once you decide to go contrary to the law of God, you lose peace. You're guilty. You're frustrated. Then you become resentful and bitter.

There's another odd thing happening today. The Church is accused of not being compassionate, and rashly judging people by telling them that this particular action is sinful. It alienates you from God, and takes away your peace. So you are no longer a peacemaker. You don't want peace, you want fun. But fun can only last so long. And when it's over, there's bitterness, terrible bitterness. And so you have to make peace with God. You have to repent. You have to repent and stay away from sin. The Church *is* compassionate because She is telling you how to make peace so that you can be a child of God. The Church is not rashly judging when She says that if you do these things, you alienate yourself from God. That is Her *duty*. That is why She is here—to tell us how to make peace; how to be blessed by God; how to be peacemakers; how to be called children of God; how to be real sons and daughters of God. Because He lives in me. But He does not live in you when you have grievous sin. You cannot be presumptuous. There is a tremendous amount of presumption today. It seems to me, in some areas, people are taught to be presumptuous. "Oh, God is compassionate," they say. "Go out and have some fun." That is such a deception, that is such a lie. God is compassionate, yes—toward the repentant. You can never make peace if you don't make peace in your own heart with God and decide you are going to live a holy life and a good life; that you are going to keep to His Word and His commandments, even if it costs you your life.

Maybe self-control is not the easiest thing in world. You may have short-lived misery, but you are going to have tremendous eternal happiness. You see, the reason you are called a "child of God" is because grace pours into your heart the more you open yourself up to peace, to repentance, to some real sorrow for your sins. And if I don't make my peace with God, I am not going to make my peace with my neighbor. That is a fallacy. Because the anger inside of you — the guilt inside of you — is manifest in your looks, your eyes, your speech and your actions. And your poor neighbor takes the brunt of what's wrong with you.

I hear so many families say to me, "My child's personality is changing — and not for the good. My boy was such a good boy, such a sweet boy, so kind, compassionate and thoughtful. And yesterday he slapped his mother." You see what it is? That's a need for a peacemaker. If there is no reconciliation with God, there is no way you can be reconciled to your neighbor. No way.

So, when considering this Beatitude, don't look at it is if we're intended to run around the world making peace. Let me tell you a little thing about peace. You are never going to do it on a wholesale level. You have to do it one-to-one — *one by one*. That's how Jesus did it. The whole essence of the Bible is one-to-one, Jesus to you. You must have a peaceful spirit because you are united with God in love and you have repented. And we are constantly in need of repentance — constantly. And as you repent and you grow in the image of Jesus, you change the world.

Now, it may look awfully impossible that we have got to go out into this world with four billion people, one at a time. But that's the only way it is going to be done, my friends. One at a time. Because it is from inside of men's hearts that evil arises. That's what Jesus says. It is also from inside of a man's heart that good comes forth. Because inside the presence of Jesus has been allowed to grow and to be manifest. That kind of person is a peacemaker. And that's why you are called a child of God.

Lord God, we praise You and bless You, Father, for giving us these wondrous Beatitudes, this blueprint for us to have. There are many who have heard my voice who are alienated from Thee in some way or other; who do not know Thee or love Thee or do not care to serve Thee. I ask, Lord, that You give them grace upon grace and bring them home. Make them understand the length and the breadth and the height and the depth of Your love for them. Grant them all the grace to make peace with You, their neighbor, their family, and the world. Amen.

Let us pray the Litany of the Sacred Heart of Jesus:

Heart of Jesus, Son of the Eternal Father,
have mercy on us.
Heart of Jesus, formed by the Holy Spirit in the womb of
the Virgin Mother,
have mercy on us.
Heart of Jesus, substantially united to the Word of God,
have mercy on us.
Heart of Jesus, of Infinite Majesty,
have mercy on us.
Heart of Jesus, Sacred Temple of God,
have mercy on us.
Heart of Jesus, Tabernacle of the Most High,
have mercy on us.
Heart of Jesus, House of God and Gate of Heaven,
have mercy on us.
Heart of Jesus, burning furnace of charity,
have mercy on us.
Heart of Jesus, abode of justice and love,
have mercy on us.
Heart of Jesus, full of goodness and love,
have mercy on us.
Heart of Jesus, abyss of all virtues,
have mercy on us.
Heart of Jesus, most worthy of all praise,
have mercy on us.

A Holy Hour with Mother Angelica

Heart of Jesus, King and center of all hearts,
have mercy on us.
Heart of Jesus, in Whom are all treasures of wisdom
 and knowledge,
have mercy on us.
Heart of Jesus, in Whom dwells the fullness of divinity,
have mercy on us.
Heart of Jesus, in Whom the Father was well pleased,
have mercy on us.
Heart of Jesus, of Whose fullness we have all received,
have mercy on us.
Heart of Jesus, desire of the everlasting hills,
have mercy on us.
Heart of Jesus, patient and most merciful,
have mercy on us.
Heart of Jesus, enriching all who invoke Thee,
have mercy on us.
Heart of Jesus, fountain of life and holiness,
have mercy on us.
Heart of Jesus, propitiation for our sins,
have mercy on us.
Heart of Jesus, loaded down with opprobrium,
have mercy on us.
Heart of Jesus, bruised for our offenses,
have mercy on us.
Heart of Jesus, obedient to death,
have mercy on us.
Heart of Jesus, pierced with a lance,
have mercy on us.
Heart of Jesus, source of all consolation,
have mercy on us.

Heart of Jesus, our life and resurrection,
have mercy on us.
Heart of Jesus, our peace and our reconciliation,
have mercy on us.
Heart of Jesus, victim for our sins,
have mercy on us.
Heart of Jesus, salvation of those who trust in Thee,
have mercy on us.
Heart of Jesus, hope of those who die in Thee,
have mercy on us.
Heart of Jesus, delight of all the Saints,
have mercy on us.

Let's look at St. Luke's Gospel (Luke 6:22–23). Luke has something about the Beatitudes that I don't want you to forget. "Blessed shall you be when men hate you, and when they shut you out, and reproach you, and reject your name as evil, because of the Son of Man. Rejoice on that day and exalt, for behold our reward is great in Heaven."

That would be like if somebody called in and said to me, "Mother Angelica, you are a first-class nut," and I said "Woohoo!" I think you would think I *was* kind of a nut and maybe the man *was* right. But that is what is in this Gospel. That we should be so rejoicing in our heart and mind and soul that we have been found worthy to suffer, to be abused, to be driven out for the sake of His Word. And in order to obtain that grace, and to persevere in it, we need to pray to the great Archangel, St. Michael:

Holy Michael the Archangel, defend us in battle. Be our protection against the wickedness and snares of the devil. May God rebuke him, we humbly pray, and do thou, O Prince of the Heavenly Host, by Divine Power thrust into Hell Satan and all the other evil spirits who wander through the world seeking the ruin of souls. Amen.

A Holy Hour with Mother Angelica

The Beatitudes are your blueprint. If you have ever asked how you can be holy, then this is God's blueprint for you. Read the Beatitudes over and over. Study them. Ask Jesus to give you grace and peace, give you that gentleness that is not weakness but great strength — to make you thirst and hunger for God and holiness. To make you a peacemaker. To make you poor in spirit, so detached and so alive to the presence of God within you and around you and in your neighbor that you have that serenity of soul that so necessary.

May the Lord God watch over you and keep you. May the Lord let His face shine upon you. May He unveil His face and His glory to you and grant you His peace. And may the Almighty God bless you in the name of the Father, the Son, and the Holy Spirit. Amen.

These Holy Hours are a spiritual lift for all of us. It is a time of the week when you just need to pray with someone. So many live alone. Some are widows and widowers. Some live alone even though there is somebody else in the house. And these Holy Hours are an opportunity to pray with someone. Jesus said, "For where two or three are gathered together for My sake, there I am in the midst of them" (Matthew 18:20). So in your living room, in your little lonely apartment, during these Holy Hours, we are here talking about the Lord and sharing our thoughts and praying. God is right here. I want you to think of that during these Holy Hours and realize that it is not fancy, it is not imaginative — it is real. He is present in our midst. That One we love, the One we work for, the One that we do all that we can for, is in our midst, is in your heart.

God bless!

Chapter 16

"The Parable of the Sower"

We are going to look at the Gospel of St. Matthew, the very first Gospel in the New Testament.

When I was a young sister, I would sometimes open up the Scriptures — you know how you do this, too; sometimes you open up the Scriptures and see if the Lord has a word for you. Well, many times, you get kind of a blank page. But I would say about eighty percent of the time, I would open up to the same parable, and that is the one of the Sower who went out to sow his seed. I just drained that thing dry. (At least, I thought I did.) It got to a point where I would meditate on the periods and commas. And then it got a little aggravating. After a while I'd say, "Lord, what are you trying to tell me?" It just was over my head. So I went to see Cardinal Manning one day in Los Angeles, and we chitchatted about the network. It must have been about three years ago. I was walking out and he had his hand on the doorknob, and he stopped and turned around to me. He said, "Remember the parable of the Sower and the seed." And I thought, "Oh yes." He said, "Do you know what the Sower did?" I said, "Well, he sowed his seed." He said, "He broadcast his seed. He *broadcast* his seed." And he said, "That's what God wants you to do — broadcast the Word!"

St. Matthew writes, "On that day Jesus left the house and was sitting on the water's edge" (Matthew 13:1). The Gospel continues:

"And as great crowds gathered about Him, He got into a boat and sat down. And all the crowd stood on the shore" (13:2).

You must use your imagination when you read Scripture; it is so much better to see Jesus in your mind as you read this. Jesus is sitting by the lakeside, just sitting down looking at the water.

Crowds gathered around Him, and so He had to get into a boat. Not to get away from the crowd, but to allow space for the crowds that could not hear Him. The people stood on the beach and He talked to them. Can you imagine what an awesome thing it must have been? What a magnetism He must've had that just attracted people to Him—what a charism—that just made those people even forget to eat.

The Lord said, "Imagine." He wants you to use your imagination. He said to imagine a sower going out to sow his seed. When you read this, it would be nice to stop and imagine in your mind a sower: "Behold the Sower went out to sow." So, stop at this point, and instead of going on any further, just imagine in your mind a sower, and he's going out and sowing his seed.

"And as he sowed, some seeds fell by the wayside, and the birds came and ate them up" (Matthew 13:4). You can imagine when somebody takes seed out of a big bag and throws it this way that some is going fall by the wayside. Other seeds fell on patches of rock and found a little soil and sprang up straightaway, meaning immediately. But there was no soil depth, so they died.

The Gospel tells us, "And other seeds fell on rocky ground, where they had not much earth; and they sprang up at once, because they had no depth of earth; but when the sun rose, they were scorched, and because they had no root they withered away. And other seeds fell among thorns; and the thorns grew up and choked them. And other seeds fell upon good ground, and yielded fruit, some a hundredfold, some sixtyfold, and some thirtyfold. He who has ears to hear, let him hear!" (Matthew 13:5–9).

So, what is He saying? Well, I think there are many things here in the Word of God that we could look at. The Word of God is sown in your heart, in your field. Your field is your soul, your mind, your intellect. It is sown every day—every moment of the day—by events, by people. But most of all, it is sown when you *read* the Word of God. And don't worry if you can't memorize the Word, or you do not remember after you have read. If you have planted it in your memory, the Spirit will bring it out when you need it. It's up to you to sow the seed. That's why it is so necessary to read the Scriptures. The Word that is in this Scripture must be sown by you in your own heart, in your own mind, by reading and by listening to the Gospel. And then remember that you, in turn, must broadcast that same Word to your neighbor—by example, by love, by compassion, by understanding. Talk about Jesus. Don't be afraid to talk about Jesus and Mary. You know, there is going to come a day, my friends, when Jesus and Mary are all you've got. Those of you who are elderly, you know that already. You may have raised nine children. They are all gone. Oh, they call you on Mother's Day and say, "Hi, Mom. I'm so grateful. Did you get my box of candy?" What about the rest of the day and the rest of the year? Who do you have but Jesus? And that's the way it should be. There's no injustice done to you. God is preparing all of us for that marvelous day when we shall be very, very much alone. We call it death. It's a glorious day, really. Because we will see then whether we have reaped a hundredfold or sixtyfold or thirtyfold. We shall understand.

You know, the Lord has taught me so much. I was going to Atlanta one day and I passed a big farm, and there was a young man on a tractor sowing seed. And it was a strange phenomenon. Suddenly he turned around and, when he turned, his wheel turned. And you know, they have these big tractors, and in that the whole field, the lines were straight as an arrow. But when he did that, that machine just turned a little bit, and where he turned it was all out of kilter. And then he turned right back again, facing straight ahead, and the lines, once again, were as perfect as could be. Perfect lines.

That is another lesson the Lord taught me about this. The Lord said to me, "Angelica, did you see what happened when he turned that tractor around?" I said, "Yes, Lord I did see." You see, you can never look back when you sow your seed. Don't turn around, don't look back. And at the time I needed to know that, because I was sowing a lot of seeds to have a Monday prayer group. It wasn't really a prayer group as much as a kind of Scripture class that I gave to Episcopalians, Methodists, and Baptists, and I used to wonder each time I spoke to them if I had said the right thing. "I wonder if they understood. I wonder, wonder, wonder," I would think. And Our Lord made very clear to me that I was going to spoil the row, I was going to mess that whole thing up if I didn't keep my eyes forward as I sowed seeds. The Lord did not want me to worry about how it fell, or where it fell, or how much fruit it bore. He just wanted me to sow the seed. And that's how it is sometimes with your children. You know you are sowing good seed. You might say, "I have sowed good seed in my children, I have brought them up Catholic. I have brought them up in the Church. They went to Catholic school. They went to Catholic college. Now they left the Faith. They left God. They're nearly atheists." Remember, though, that their memory is like a computer. Every seed you sow is still there. It's a marvel. One day, your example, your smile, your love, your compassion, your patience will all come back and the Spirit will bring it back to them. The seed you sow today may not bear fruit for a while. It may look like it's all choked up and pulled out. But that seed has been sown in a computer that we call a memory. And the Lord's Spirit will bring it out, maybe when you are in the Heavenly Kingdom, and that child will be saved; that child will know God. You must have that total confidence in the Sower who sows seeds through you. *He sows seeds through you.* Leave it to Him to bear the fruit. Don't worry about it. Don't look back. Keep your eyes forward to what is coming next, not looking backward on what's been accomplished; not on what you have done; or not on what He's done in you, through you, or with you — only on the unplowed field ahead. To the whole field of the earth — the world — that has yet to hear the word of God.

Lord God, I praise You and bless You for making all of us sowers of seed — for asking us to broadcast that seed. Give us the grace, Lord, not to look back but to keep our eyes riveted on the unplowed field ahead, with all the rocks and the hard ground and soil. And send water into the soil, Lord. Send the water of Thy Spirit so that the seed we broadcast by example, by media of every form, by love and compassion, might bear great fruit. We ask this in the name of Jesus and Mary. Amen.

Let us say this Litany of His Most Holy Name:

Jesus, Son of the living God,
have mercy on us.
Jesus, Splendor of the Father,
have mercy on us.
Jesus, Brightness of eternal Light,
have mercy on us.
Jesus, King of Glory,
have mercy on us.
Jesus, Sun of Justice,
have mercy on us.
Jesus, Son of the Virgin Mary,
have mercy on us.

A Holy Hour with Mother Angelica

Jesus, most amiable,

have mercy on us.

Jesus, most admirable,

have mercy on us.

Jesus, the mighty God,

have mercy on us.

Jesus, Father of the world to come,

have mercy on us.

Jesus, angel of great counsel,

have mercy on us.

Jesus, most powerful,

have mercy on us.

Jesus, most patient,

have mercy on us.

Jesus, most obedient,

have mercy on us.

Jesus, meek and humble of heart,

have mercy on us.

Jesus, Lover of Chastity,

have mercy on us.

Jesus, our Lover,

have mercy on us.

Jesus, God of Peace,

have mercy on us.

Jesus, Author of Life,

have mercy on us.

Jesus, Model of Virtues,

have mercy on us.

Jesus, zealous for souls,

have mercy on us.

Jesus, our God,

have mercy on us.

Jesus, our Refuge,
have mercy on us.
Jesus, Father of the Poor,
have mercy on us.
Jesus, Treasure of the Faithful,
have mercy on us.
Jesus, good Shepherd,
have mercy on us.
Jesus, true Light,
have mercy on us.
Jesus, eternal Wisdom,
have mercy on us.
Jesus, infinite Goodness,
have mercy on us.
Jesus, our Way and our Life,
have mercy on us.
Jesus, joy of the Angels,
have mercy on us.
Jesus, King of the Patriarchs,
have mercy on us.
Jesus, Master of the Apostles,
have mercy on us.
Jesus, Teacher of the Evangelists,
have mercy on us.
Jesus, Strength of Martyrs,
have mercy on us.
Jesus, Light of Confessors,
have mercy on us.
Jesus, Purity of Virgins,
have mercy on us.
Jesus, Crown of all Saints,
have mercy on us.

A Holy Hour with Mother Angelica

Let us pray. Lord Jesus Christ, You have said, "Ask and you shall receive; seek and you shall find; knock and it shall be opened to you"; mercifully attend to our supplications, and grant us the grace of Your most divine love, that we love You with all our hearts, and in all our words and actions, and never cease to praise You.

Make us, O Lord, to have a perpetual fear and love of Your holy name, for You never fail to govern those whom You establish in Your love. You, Who live and reign forever and ever. Amen.

Let us read Psalm 119:105–110 (RSVCE):

Thy Word is a lamp to my feet and a light to my path.
O Lord give me life according to Your Word;
I have sworn an oath and confirmed it,
To observe Thy righteous ordinances.
I am sorely afflicted;
Give me life, O Lord, according to Thy Word!
Accept my offerings of praise, O Lord,
And teach me Thy ordinances.
I hold my life in my hand continually,
But I do not forget Thy law.
The wicked have laid a snare for me,
But I do not stray from Thy precepts.

We have talked a lot about sowing seed and bearing fruit. Once you sow the seed, whether it's in your heart or the heart of your neighbor, the Lord bears fruit. Remember, the Lord said once that without Him, we can do nothing. That's a pretty big statement. We need to pray that we realize that without Jesus we cannot accomplish anything. So ask the Lord every day to give you humility of heart, that we can know with all our weaknesses that although there are times when we don't even bear a little fruit, still we have borne some, and still there is that seed that is struggling to break through the ground. But it is growing, so let's never be disheartened.

Holy Michael, the Archangel, defend us in battle. Be our protection against the wickedness and snares of the devil. May God rebuke him, we humbly pray, and do thou, O Prince of the Heavenly Host, by Divine Power thrust into Hell Satan and all the other evil spirits who wander through the world seeking the ruin of souls. Amen.

As we read about sowing seeds, what are we sowing for? The Kingdom of God, and we're living inside the Kingdom. That's so important, but what does it mean to "live in the Kingdom?" What kind of seed is to be sown that will enable us to live in the Kingdom? The greatest seed of all, the seed of His awesome presence planted into our hearts at Baptism — and don't ever forget those seeds of faith and hope and love. Through faith, I see God in the present moment, be it ever so painful. Through hope, I know He brings good out of everything that happens to me — *everything*. Even my creaky bones in rainy weather. And out of love I see the merciful love of Jesus in my life where He forgives me every day, a thousand times a day. And so the seed that you and I are to bring forth is the same seed planted in us at Baptism. That is that seed of the divine presence. If I live in the presence of Jesus, I might stray a little bit to distractions, anxieties, and frustration. Calmly, calmly now, not full of frustration, but calmly, draw yourself back into that awesome presence. Just close your eyes. You say, "Every time I close my eyes, all I see is darkness." Oh no. All you see is that closet that Jesus spoke about. He said, "go in your closet and shut the door" (Matthew 6:6). Well, go into your closet and shut the door and see what happens. It's dark in there, but it's very quiet.

A Holy Hour with Mother Angelica

Be an evangelist. Go get 'em. Just go out there and say, "Hey, do you know God loves you?" Oh, you've planted a seed. You'll be surprised how many people say, "What? God loves *me*? But, I'm a sinner. I'm awful. I'm this and that." And you can reply, "No, God loves you." How do you like that, huh? I think that's the best news that you could sell. Broadcast that kind of news. Show some enthusiasm. How would you like it if somebody came up and said, "God loves you; He really does. I mean He loves you a lot. You ought to think about it"? If you say this to people, they might say, "What kind of love is that?"

You're the mirror of Jesus, so be a bright mirror. Can you do that? And tell somebody, somewhere, "Hey, God loves you," and you'll be surprised the reaction you'll get. No matter what kind of reaction it is, it will always be surprising.

I love you, too.

Chapter 17

"Fraternal Correction, Forgiveness, and Healing"

We are going to look at St. Matthew's Gospel. I think it's one of the most misrepresented and misunderstood counsels of Our Lord in this day and age. It boggles the mind. Our Lord begins by saying, "But if thy brother sins against thee, go and show him his fault, between thee and him alone" (18:15).

We're scared. We're chickens. You know what we all need? Fear of the Lord. Not the servile fear that's simply afraid of going to Hell, but the kind that says, "The Lord is my Father and He has told me not to do a certain thing. And I am not going to do it. It ruins my soul. It ruins my body. It ruins my mind. It defiles the temple of the Holy Spirit."

Today, we have taken away God from our lives. It's so sad when I see dissenting priests and religious persons on television, for example. I think you and I need to make reparation for all of these dissenters going up on television, all these people who have such hatred for the Holy Father and everything Catholic and every moral and faith-filled counsel and law—the Law of God, the Ten Commandments. They have thrown them away, and these people give you license to go to Hell. These are people who have no respect for God's Vicar because they don't believe in God's Vicar. I would keep my mouth shut if I believed what they believed. Do not prevent other people from going to the Kingdom because you don't want to go. I think we need to be able to say to these kinds of people that they are wrong.

But you can't go to these people privately. Most of them, you don't know who they are or what they're doing and, all of a sudden, you just see them on television. The fact that they're on television means that millions of viewers are now confused, and maybe their souls are in danger as well. Their souls are in danger because they, too, follow like sheep, but they follow the wrong shepherd. They follow a wolf in sheep's clothing.

You and I must be able today to watch all those who dissent. Not those who are willing just to disagree and sit around the table and have it out, but those who go public. It's such a lack of respect, so much insult and rudeness. Have we lost respect? Is it because we have ceased to correct our neighbor that we have lost the concept of what is right and what is wrong because of our fear of correction?

The Lord says go alone. "If he listens to thee, thou hast won thy brother." But Jesus knew sometimes that was not going to work. So He said, "But if he do not listen to thee, take with thee one or two more so that on the word of two or three witnesses every word may be confirmed" (18:15–16).

See, the Lord doesn't believe in just letting things go. So He said, "And, if he refuses to hear even the Church, let him be to thee as the heathen and the publican. Amen, I say to you, whatever you bind on earth shall be bound also in heaven, and whatever you loose on earth shall be loosed also in heaven" (18:17–18).

He is to be treated like a pagan or a tax collector! Those are harsh words to our minds today, because we have lost the reality of sin. We really don't know what happens to our brother when we sin. And when he sins, we don't think of the consequences. It's like we have obliterated Heaven, Hell, Purgatory, and God from the face of the earth. And we say today, as clearly as it was said ages ago, "I will not serve." And you know, a lot of us are in that position because we refuse to admit there is such a thing as sin or authority or just plain politeness. We refuse to admit that those things even exist. As a result, we have uncontrolled tempers, un-controlled actions, uncontrolled lives, uncontrolled thoughts and actions. The whole thing is just totally out of control, so we think that whoever disagrees with us is a nobody.

Considering that Our Holy Father John Paul II was on the receiving end of so much of the vitriol, I offered this prayer for his protection against so many who would greet him with hatred:

Lord, I ask pardon for all our sins, our disobedience, our rebellious nature. I ask pardon, Lord, and I ask that Your Vicar may be protected from the enemy—protected from those who do not understand his compassion or Your Law. Who treat him very much like the old prophets when the people said to them, "We do not want to hear what you have to say! We close our ears to your voice." Lord God, open our ears, give us light to see, give us light to obey, give us light to understand. Give us the Christian politeness at least to listen. That we may make all things new. Amen.

Let us pray a Litany of the Divine Mercy:

Divine Mercy, gushing forth from the bosom of the Father,
I trust in You.
Divine Mercy, greatest attribute of God,
I trust in You.
Divine Mercy, incomprehensible mystery,
I trust in You.
Divine Mercy, unfathomed by any intellect, human or
angelic,
I trust in You.

A Holy Hour with Mother Angelica

Divine Mercy, from Which wells forth all life and
    happiness,
I trust in You.
Divine Mercy, better than the Heavens,
I trust in You.
Divine Mercy, source of miracles and wonders,
I trust in You.
Divine Mercy, Which flowed out from the open wound of
    the Heart of Jesus,
I trust in You.
Divine Mercy, unfathomed in the Institution of the Sa-
    cred Host,
I trust in You.
Divine Mercy, in the Sacrament of Baptism,
I trust in You.
Divine Mercy, in the Sacrament of Penance,
I trust in You.
Divine Mercy, accompanying us through our whole life,
I trust in You.
Divine Mercy, embracing us, especially at the hour of our
    death,
I trust in You.
Divine Mercy, in the conversion of hardened sinners,
I trust in You.
Divine Mercy, lifting us out of every misery,
I trust in You.
Divine Mercy, source of our happiness and joy,
I trust in You.
Divine Mercy, embracing all the works of Jesus' hands,
I trust in You.
Divine Mercy, crown of all of God's handiwork,
I trust in You.

Divine Mercy, sweet relief of anguished hearts,
I trust in You.
Divine Mercy, repose of hearts in peace amidst fear,
I trust in You.
Divine Mercy, delight and ecstasy of holy souls,
I trust in You.
Divine Mercy, inspiring hope in times of despair,
I trust in You.

Let us pray. Eternal God, in Whom mercy is endless and the treasury of compassion inexhaustible, look kindly upon us, and increase Your mercy in us that in difficult moments we might not despair nor become despondent, but with great confidence submit ourselves to Your holy will, which is love and mercy itself. Amen.

You know, our Lord is trying to say to us, "I want you to forgive," so He gives us that parable about the steward who owed his master quite a bit of money. Altogether, I think it would have equaled nine million dollars. So, let's say I owe Bill nine million dollars. I'd say, "Oh, Bill, I can't pay you. I just don't have it." And Bill would say, "It's okay. I'll just forget it. I'll write it off." Can you beat that? Can you even imagine it? And then let's say Joe comes to me and he owes me fifteen dollars, and, I say to him, "Pay up!" And he says, "Well, Mother, I don't have fifteen dollars," and I would say, "Well you go out and work in the ditches until you pay me that money!" That is the picture the Lord is giving us as a motivation for forgiving. You know, if we are going to be forgiven, we have got to forgive as many times as we are forgiven. And how many times a day is that? Only God knows, because we do so many things that need forgiveness, that need the healing power of forgiveness. I think that this is clever, the way the Lord tells us this in the story.

A Holy Hour with Mother Angelica

I think if we understood that even with that parable of the beam and the splinter, the Lord still encourages us to correct. He tells us to look at ourselves, but still He gives you leave to correct others. In fact, He said to Peter one day that once you have been converted, *then* convert your brother. This is because Peter, having been forgiven a big sin, could then forgive his brother seventy times seven times a day.

In today's world especially we need to pray the St. Michael prayer that Pope Leo XVIII asked us to pray so often for protection from the enemy who inspires so much rebellion and the lack of a forgiving spirit. We seem to think that it's better to let it go or just to become very resentful and very guilty. Let us pray:

Holy Michael, the Archangel, defend us in battle. Be our protection against the wickedness and snares of the devil. May God rebuke him, we humbly pray, and do thou, O Prince of the Heavenly Host, by Divine Power thrust into Hell Satan and all the other evil spirits who wander through the world seeking the ruin of souls. Amen.

You know sometimes I say to the sisters, "Watch out for human truth and seek Divine Truth." This is because human truth would say, "Well it did hurt me and it was unjustified, so I have every reason not to forgive." You know, the truth sometimes keeps us from forgiving because maybe it *was* very unjust. I think if we observed this one thing, we would be asking forgiveness before we went to bed. Don't let the sun go down on your anger. Obviously, that's one of the key solutions to the whole problem. And the worst about that is that you take it out on people around you, people that did not even know what was wrong. I mean, they did not do anything to you, and you have gotten so caught up in it and built it up in your head that the first person that comes up that does some little insignificant thing, you just chew their head off. They just look and say, "What's wrong with you?" They don't know the seething inside of you. So you can see why our Lord was so wise in telling us not to let the sun go down on our anger. And in the summer time, you've got an extra hour of daylight with Daylight Savings Time, too, so you have even longer to make amends.

If only we would forgive each other, what a country we would have!

Let us pray that the Church will have a forgiving spirit, that those of us who have a hard time forgiving will obtain from God His love and His mercy. God bless you.

Chapter 18

"More Repentance"

Before we begin any kind of prayer or Holy Hour, we need to call ourselves to repentance. I know that's not very a popular word today because we want so much for there to be no sin. It would not be too bad if we wished that, because we do not want God to be offended. But we just do not want to admit that there exists a sin, or that we commit sin. It's kind of a guilt thing—but it isn't, you see. If you do something wrong you must say, "I am sorry." That's all repentance is. It's saying, "Lord, I admit my offense. I am sorry I offended You, and because You are so good and You deserve better from me, I ask forgiveness." That isn't hard to do. But we find it hard to do.

Lord God, give me the light to see myself as You see me. Give me the courage to accept that self-knowledge. Give me the humility to accept it. Give me the zeal to want to change my life, to have a conversion experience. Lord, give me that desire to change, without which I cannot make that necessary change. Give me a thirst for holiness even as I sit here, a sinner. Give me the desire to be holy so that I can make my repentance with a pure love—a love that is not only sorry for having offended Thee, but sorry because I deserve any kind of punishment and I am willing to accept that punishment provided I do not offend You again. So, give me the resolution and the determination not to commit these sins over and over and over. Let me see myself, Lord. Let me see my neighbor as they are. Let me see the good in my neighbor. Give me Your grace, Lord, moment to moment. Give me the desire to be holy as You are holy.

Let us look at St. Mark's Gospel, after John the Baptist had been arrested. We know why John the Baptist was arrested: he was too honest, too truthful; he wasn't afraid to say to Herod, "It is not lawful for thee to have thy brother's wife" (see Mark 6:18). So Herod had him arrested. I mean, who wants to be told they're doing something wrong in public? And there John the Baptist proclaimed the Good News from God. "The time is fulfilled, and the Kingdom of God is at hand," he said. "Repent and believe in the gospel" (see 1:15). Surely Herod had heard the Good News!

Now, some of you are going to think, "Well, he said it was close at hand. That was almost two thousand years ago and nothing's happened so far. I've got lots of time." Oh, don't you kid yourself. I don't think we have lots of time. Read the signs of the times and you will find, my friends, we do not have lots of time, because we do not even know what it means to repent. If I say, "I'm sorry," and I say to God, "I repent," that's great. But as a Catholic, I must go to Confession. I must accept the Sacrament of Reconciliation. I must hear the words from God Himself: "I absolve you from all your sins." And the unfortunate part today is that the Sacrament of Confession, as practiced, resembles nothing of the Sacrament that Jesus instituted.

I recently heard about a woman who went to Confession. (At least she *thought* she was going to Confession.) And the priest said to her, "Have you made an Examination of Conscience?" And she said yes. He then said, "I'll just give you the absolution and I'll say your penance for you." I've never heard of such a ridiculous thing in my life! And believe me, Sweetheart, I wouldn't want to say anybody's penance for them. That's no confession. That's a mockery. You've got to say your sins. You really have to want to be sorry for your sins. You have to have the desire never to offend God in that area again. You just can't make a mockery of the Sacraments. You can't change morality to fit your situation.

I'm just reading St. Mark's Gospel 1:15, which says, "Repent and believe. The Kingdom of Heaven is close at hand." And you know, my friends, we have brought upon ourselves chastisements in the past. Every World War was a chastisement that God permitted. We brought it on ourselves through our greed, our ambition, our desire for other people's property and land and everything else. We exploit people. We exploit nations and then we look at God and say, "Hey, You're chastising us." When God lets us go, we chastise ourselves. And when we say, "I repent," we're not just saying, "I'm sorry"; we're saying, "I want to change my life." Because believing the Good News goes hand in hand with repentance. That's what the Lord said through St. John the Baptist: "Repent and believe the good news." I need not only to repent, I need to change my life. I need to believe!

What does it mean to believe the Good News? It doesn't mean that you *know* the Good News. He didn't say, "Repent and know the Good News." He said, "believe." If you believe anything, you are going to live it. And people believe in a lot of things. They believe in diets. Oh, do they believe in exercise! They're jogging themselves to death. They believe in political parties to the point of fighting. These political conventions are really something. People give their bodies, their souls — everything they've got — to the party. Why do you do that? Why do you go without sleep? Why do you just push yourself for this party? "I believe in it," you say. Oh, so belief and action go together. You cannot believe in Jesus without fighting for Jesus, without living the life that Jesus wants for you. Otherwise you are a liar. That's what St. John the Baptist says. Believing is doing. So, when Jesus says to repent, you must do what Jesus wants you to do: you must be like Jesus.

A Holy Hour with Mother Angelica

I know a book called *Catholic Christians or Christian Catholics*. It's not worth the paper it's written on. Why? Because it says that Catholics believe in the *possibility* of Hell. Let me tell you, Sweetheart: don't you let anyone tell you that. There *is* a Hell. And there *is* a Heaven. And you have to choose which one you are going to. You can't live two different kinds of lives. A person who lives two different kinds of lives is a person the Lord calls a hypocrite. We can't say one thing and then do something else because, you see, if you do that, you lack repentance and you do not believe the Good News.

And so we have to take a hold of ourselves today. We really do. I am not saying you have to go out and put on sackcloth and ashes like the people that Jonah had to preach to did. But I am saying we need to put on the *sackcloth of repentance* and the *ashes of humility* and to cry out to God, "Lord, this nation and my family and my own self and my neighbors — all of us have sinned against You and Heaven and we are sorry." Does that take a lot? Is that too much to ask? If we don't do that, I can tell you those angels are going to start blowing those horns and pouring out those bowls. And when they do, you are going to see fireworks.

"Oh, Mother, that scares me," you say. "I don't want to hear that." Well, it doesn't have to happen. The angels don't have to clean up the world if we clean it up first — if we repent, if we pray.

We have to pray for poor sinners. People are committing suicide. Our youth are falling into despair. I guess the worst kind of suicide is a kind of indifference, saying "I don't care." It's a kind of spiritual suicide. I don't think the only suicide in the world is the kind where people destroy the body. I think it's also when you give up on your faith, you give up on God, you give up on your Church, you give up on society. It's a kind of hopelessness that just drains all the love and grace and virtue right out of you. It makes you live Hell on earth. And Jesus doesn't want that. He did not come to make things harder for us. He came to make them easier. He came so that you and I would love one another.

I heard of a little boy who was, for the first four years of his life, kept in one room, locked up. Locked up for four years! You can't imagine parents doing that. And when they did find him, he was all bruised. What kind of society do we live in if we have no care for each other, no love for each other? Do you know why this happens? Because we don't repent. We don't feel sorry. We don't ask for forgiveness.

There is a lot that hinges on repentance, an awful lot. If I am sorry, I am going to be patient with my neighbor. Why? Because I know I am a sinner. I cannot afford to be impatient with my neighbor. When I know God looks at me, He does not see anything much better. Not only does He know what I can do, He knows everything I would do in every possible situation. And none of it may be too good. So if I do not have self-knowledge and I do not repent, I am not going to be patient with my neighbor. Everybody is going to be in the way. Even your children become burdens, or your parents, or your husband or your wife become burdens. Repentance is the absolute foundation of our spiritual life. It does not mean putting on sackcloth and ashes and wearing purple. It means that my heart is repentant and then I am going to have mercy on my brother, because I know where I come from; I know who I am; I know what I am capable of. If you know that about yourself, you are not going to be impatient with your brother.

So when we say we repent, we are not just saying, "Hey, let's be sorry for a few sins." It's very deep in the heart. I am not going to have compassion for my neighbor if I never say I'm sorry to God, because then I become hard, I demand what I cannot do. I make demands on people to do things that I myself don't do. This lack of compassion is why I have never said to God, "I am sorry for the things I don't do." I would never find fault with someone for their imperfections if I realized that I, too, don't do the right thing at the right time in the right place. Sometimes I am also guilty of omissions—of not doing all of the things that could be done for my neighbor.

So there are all kinds of repentance—there are all kinds of ways of saying "I'm sorry" to God. Because if you don't repent, your own soul gets eaten up. Then you spew out on society and your parents and your relatives and your neighbors and the people you work with all this inner venom that has never been released, never been cleansed, that you have never gotten rid of. So you take it out on other people because they remind you of yourself. You don't want to see your own faults. Why not? Because you have never admitted to the Lord God that you are a sinner and that you need forgiveness and you need to change.

There is a short paragraph in the Gospel of Mark. It's very short, but it has a lot of power in it. We often don't look at real repentance and how far-reaching it is into our lives and how it affects other people. My lack of repentance affects everybody around me. My lack of self-knowledge interferes with my union with God. So, think about it, will you? Think and see perhaps how your relationship with your husband, your wife, your children, your family, your relatives—those you work with, those you live with—is affected by your lack of self-knowledge; your lack of repentance and a lack of humility; and your lack of compassion. So when we do say, "I repent," it's much deeper and more important than we realize.

As long as you have a loving, repentant heart, you can be assured of God's love and mercy.

Lord God, we praise You and bless You.
Lord, we ask for the gift of repentance, the gift of self-knowledge, and the gift of courage—that we may not take

out on others what is within our own hearts; that we may look only to Thee for forgiveness and grace; and reach out to our neighbor in love, patience, compassion, without which we cannot love.

So, we ask these graces, Lord, on all of us, that we may stop long enough in this hurried world to say, "Lord God, Father, we have sinned against Thee in Heaven and against man on earth." Forgive us. Give us the grace to be holy as You are holy. We ask this in the name, the powerful name, of Jesus, who is Lord of All. Amen.

Let us pray the Litany of the Most Precious Blood of Jesus:

Blood of Christ, only-begotten Son of the Eternal
   Father,
save us.
Blood of Christ, Incarnate Word of God,
save us.
Blood of Christ, of the New and Eternal Testament,
save us.
Blood of Christ, falling upon the earth in the Agony,
save us.
Blood of Christ, shed profusely in the Scourging,
save us.
Blood of Christ, flowing forth in the Crowning with
   Thorns,
save us.
Blood of Christ, poured out on the Cross,
save us.
Blood of Christ, price of our salvation,
save us.
Blood of Christ, without which there is no forgiveness,
save us.

A Holy Hour with Mother Angelica

Blood of Christ, Eucharistic drink and refreshment
of souls,
save us.
Blood of Christ, stream of mercy,
save us.
Blood of Christ, victor over demons,
save us.
Blood of Christ, courage of Martyrs,
save us.
Blood of Christ, strength of Confessors,
save us.
Blood of Christ, bringing forth Virgins,
save us.
Blood of Christ, help of those in peril,
save us.
Blood of Christ, relief of the burdened,
save us.
Blood of Christ, solace in sorrow,
save us.
Blood of Christ, hope of the penitent,
save us.
Blood of Christ, consolation of the dying,
save us.
Blood of Christ, peace and tenderness of hearts,
save us.
Blood of Christ, pledge of eternal life,
save us.
Blood of Christ, freeing souls from purgatory,
save us.
Blood of Christ, most worthy of all glory and honor,
save us.

Let us pray. Almighty and eternal God, You have appointed Your only-begotten Son the Redeemer of the world, and willed to be appeased by His Blood. Grant we beg of You, that we may worthily adore this price of our salvation, and through its power be safeguarded from the evils of the present life, so that we may rejoice in its fruits forever in Heaven. Through the same Christ our Lord. Amen.

The Litany of the Precious Blood! I think sometimes we forget, perhaps as Catholics anyway, to ask the Lord, ask the Spirit, to let the Precious Blood pour upon us. That's what happens at Confession, the Sacrament of Reconciliation. The Precious Blood of Jesus pours upon us. That's what happens in the Eucharist. The Precious Blood of Jesus is received into your own body and blood. And I think that sometimes we do not call upon the Precious Blood as a protection, especially in this day of evil, and with the enemy being so strong in so many ways in society and in families. It's so sad because Jesus is always there, because you can go to receive Him at any Mass. But we are not oriented towards the awesomeness of it. Somehow, we lose it. How can we keep ourselves aware? You are not always going to have feelings, you are not always going to feel the Eucharist. The Lord is not always going to talk to you after Communion. So in order to keep our fervor up—what can the average person do, a person who is going to Mass, and then has to go to work and bump heads with a hard world?

I think we need to concentrate. I think that if we said fewer prayers, sometimes, but say them really fervently, especially if we have something that we have not forgiven someone, or they haven't forgiven us for. It's hard to say, "Forgive us our trespasses as we forgive others." We kind of rattle it off as if it was just something we are supposed to say. But that is the demand that the Lord has made.

A Holy Hour with Mother Angelica

And sometimes we just think that God is way up there and we have this big job to do—and that is holiness in our work and everything else combined. We kind of look at Him as if to say, "Help me a little bit." But we often say "help me" rather than "Lord, You do it." We just have a hard time with knowing that God *wants* to do it for us. He wants to do it within us. I think maybe, as Americans, we have that "instant-itis" problem. We want everything to be instant. We are accustomed to things happening fast. We want them done right away. I myself, as an Italian, have the same problem—it's inherited, supposedly. At least I like to blame it on my heredity. But it seems to me that we do not take the time to reflect. We could use a little bit of the Eastern patience—like the Eastern Orthodox Rites, the Eastern Byzantines, and all these people who take time with their liturgies. If we are not out in a half hour, we think there's something wrong with the priest.

We spoke of repentance and the need to take upon ourselves the Blood of Jesus, and to ask for the Blood of Jesus to protect us, to guide us, to lead us, to inspire us. It's a great deterrent against the power of the enemy. If there is one thing Satan and his cohorts do not like, it's when you call upon yourself the Precious Blood of Jesus. The Son of God loved you enough to come down, to live, suffer and die an ignominious death just for you, as if no one else existed. So let us use the sacraments that Our Lord has given us and the sacramentals as well—rosaries, scapulars, Sacred Heart badges, all the things that keep reminding us of our eternal goal of Heaven and the Lord.

The Lord to bless you, and guide you, and protect you.

Chapter 19

"A Marian Holy Hour"

We are going to have a Marian Holy Hour, to speak of Mary and to speak *to* Mary. The reason we do this is because Mary is the Mother of God.

Let's look at two important chapters of the Bible. One is in St. Luke's Gospel, and one is in St. John's Gospel, and in each of these, we hear Mary's words. We see Mary and we are able to observe, by her beautiful example, what she was thinking; what her soul must have been like; what her heart must have been like; and why God chose this wondrous woman to be the promised woman.

As we prepare to continue our journey to God—and that's what these Holy Hours are all about—these Holy Hours are to aid us. They're little stop signs, little stations on our way home: and everyone is on their way home. This world is not our home. We are on our way home. This life is a pilgrimage—the pilgrimage of life is looking forward to arriving at home, that place where Jesus has gone before us to prepare a place for us. We want to be sure we get there. We know He's going to do all He can to help with all the wonderful things He will give us—His grace, His gifts, His inspiration, His guidance, His angels, His Mother, His Church—just hundreds of things He puts in our path. The problem is that you and I stumble over them sometimes; we walk around them; then we go under them, largely unaware of these gifts. So, we do not always benefit from the tremendous gifts and graces that God gives us.

So, I would like you to just say to Him, "Lord, I've messed things up. I've messed things up so bad that I do not even remember what I messed up. I know I have not corresponded to all of Your grace. I know there are many times You have asked me to do things and I've said no. I know I have deliberately walked into occasions of sin. I know I have deliberately gone to places where I know, for sure, there would be temptation. So, Lord, I have not always been the person You want me to be, but I know that You love me and that Your merciful hand is always extended toward me. And so I want to begin again. I want a new sheet, a whole new clean sheet. I want to go to Confession. I want to confess my sins, Lord. I want to receive absolution. I want to know You. I want to serve You. I want to love You."

We should also say, "Lord, teach me about Your Mother." She's the most beautiful woman. All the feminists that are so concerned about women's rights should look at this woman. Look at her, look at the most beautiful and the most wonderful woman who ever existed. She's the promised woman of Genesis.

> Lord God, give us that grace, that we may understand the role of Your Mother. We have a role in salvation history, and she had a role as well; a very definite and important role. So teach us, Lord, her role, that we may find our own role. Amen.

We are going to look at a very important aspect of our spirituality. We are always talking about doing the will of God, and we need to see how Mary, the Mother of God, did the will of God and how we do the will of God. There is a vast difference and really you can kind of access your own holiness. Everybody wants to make sure they are progressing in the spiritual life. "Am I making any kind of progress? Am I getting better?" Well, you can't be sure, but one rule of thumb is to ask yourself, "how do I accomplish the will of God? How readily, how cheerfully, and how unitedly am I working with the will of God in the present moment?" That's a pretty good test to see if we are making any kind of progress.

Now, in the first chapter of Luke, you and I are depicted quite graphically, and Mary is depicted just as graphically. If you want to find out how you can judge yourself, this would be a great example, and we find it in St. Luke's Gospel in the first chapter. Here we see Zechariah, a priest, and it was his turn to exercise his priestly office. It fell to him by lots to enter the Lord's sanctuary and to burn incense. Well, the hour of incense came along and the congregation was out there waiting, and he goes inside. Now, Zechariah is an old man and an angel of the Lord appears to him on the right of the altar of incense. Zechariah was scared to death. He's an old man, he's been offering incense, his turn has come up as it does every so often, as he has been a priest of the Lord. He's been praying, praying, praying, for a son. He and his wife have no children. In those days, you were considered cursed by God if you didn't have children.

Well, this sight disturbed Zechariah. He was overcome with fear. "But the angel said to him, 'Do not be afraid, Zechariah, for thy petition has been heard'" (Luke 1:13). What would you do if you prayed for something for thirty years? Then all of the sudden, this giant angel comes along and appears to you, and he says, "Hey, your prayer has been heard." Wouldn't you get excited?

The angel said, "Thy wife Elizabeth shall bear thee a son and thou shalt call his name John." He even gives him his name! "And thou shalt have joy and gladness, and many will rejoice at his birth. For he shall be great before the Lord" (Luke 1:13–15).

All of you people out there who don't have any children, or those who have a first son, imagine an angel saying that your son is going to be the delight of the Lord and a delight to you! And the angel said, "he shall drink no wine or strong drink, and shall be filled with the Holy Spirit even from his mother's womb" (Luke 1:15). How many of you who are pregnant wish and hope that the child in your womb would be filled with the Holy Spirit?

Well, the angel was not finished. He said, "And he shall bring back to the Lord their God many of the children of Israel, and he shall himself go before him in the spirit and power of Elias, to turn the hearts of fathers to their children and the incredulous to witness to the wisdom of the just; to prepare for the Lord a perfect people" (Luke 1:16–17). Can you imagine your tiny little baby having that kind of prophecy from an angel of the Lord? What would you do? Wouldn't you be jumping up and down?

You know what Zechariah said? He said, "How shall I know this? For I am an old man and my wife is advanced in years" (see Luke 1:18). Here is Zechariah explaining the facts of life to an angel. His wife is getting on in years — big news. And what he's really saying to this great angel is, "Sorry, buddy. You are about forty years too late. Why didn't you tell me this forty years ago?"

And, the angel was angry. So if I were you, if you ever see an angel, you be careful what you say to him. Because you know what the angel said? He replied, "I am Gabriel, who stands in the presence of God; and I have been sent to speak to thee and to bring thee this good news. And behold, thou shalt be dumb and unable to speak until the day when these things come to pass, because thou hast not believed my words, which will be fulfilled in their proper time" (Luke 1:19–20). I bet you his wife Elizabeth was tickled pink at this silence, because I would imagine that Zechariah may have been an old grump because he was disheartened, he was unhappy. His prayers had not been answered. And you can tell he's lost hope the way that he answers that angel.

Now, you may think Zechariah did a terrible thing, but you and I do this constantly. We pray for something, and if we don't get it immediately, or it doesn't come the way we want, we say, "Look, God, I know You tried." Or maybe you think, "this was too big for You," or "this really can't happen, but I'll take a crack at it, I'll pray anyway." This is a typical human reaction—this is how we pray most of the time. And this is where our will is. Our will is not in the will of God. Zechariah is being told by an angel what the will of God was and he says, "I want to be sure." How much more sure can you get?

Now I want you to look at Mary, that awesome woman. She was only about fifteen years old, if she was that. That same angel, the "angel Gabriel was sent from God to a town of Galilee called Nazareth to a virgin betrothed to a man named Joseph, of the house of David, and the virgin's name was Mary" (see Luke 1:26–27). It's very important that in the Scripture they say "virgin" twice already.

"And when the angel had come to her, he said, 'Hail Mary, full of grace, the Lord is with thee. Blessed art thou among women" (Luke 1:28). Every man, woman, and child is born with original sin. You may not like it, but that's the way it is. This, however, proved Mary was not. You say, "Oh, she was like everybody else." No, wait a minute. Remember, nothing is impossible with God. That's just what Gabriel said to Zechariah.

Now, don't be a Zechariah! Everything is possible to God. Mary had to be conceived without sin. Why? Because she was to be the spotless temple of the Son of God. Spotless. Not spotted and then bleached, but spotless. God's attributes—His Divinity—demand a spotless Ark of the Covenant. A spotless temple. Common sense tells you that. Now, why was she conceived without Original Sin? Because otherwise she could not be highly favored, she could not be filled grace, filled with God. But she was, in anticipation of her Son's redemption of the world. So, when Jesus died and suffered, He also died and suffered for the prerogatives she was given ahead of time.

"When she heard this," St. Luke writes, "she was troubled at his word, and kept pondering what manner of greeting this might be" (Luke 1:29), just like Zechariah.

So, what's the difference between Mary and Zechariah? They were both deeply disturbed. She asked herself what this greeting could mean. She asked herself, though, not the angel, because she was humble. You and I would say, "thank you very much!" She said, "Oh."

And, the angel said to her, "Do not be afraid, Mary," the same thing he said to Zechariah, "For thou hast found grace with God. Behold, thou shalt conceive in thy womb and shalt bring forth a Son; and thou shalt call His name Jesus" (Luke 1:30–31). This is almost the same thing he said to Zechariah. She would conceive, bear a Son, and gave Him the name Jesus. "He shall be great, and shall be called the Son of the Most High; and the Lord God will give Him the throne of David His father, and He shall be King over the house of Jacob forever; and His Kingdom shall have no end" (Luke 1:32–33).

Now what's the difference between Zechariah and Mary? The difference is love, trust, hope, faith. That's the difference. Zechariah said, "How can I be sure?" Mary asked, "How shall this happen?" (Luke 1:34). She had it right. Why did she have it right? Why would Mary ask the question? It says here that she said, "how can this come about, since I am a virgin?" Well she was already betrothed to Joseph and she intended to be and stay a virgin. So, she merely wanted to know how the Lord God could have her do two opposite things: conceive and bear a Son, *and* remain a virgin. The answer is right there, and you have to be pretty blind to not see it: "And the angel answered and said to her, 'The Holy Spirit shall come upon thee and the power of the Most High shall overshadow thee; and therefore the Holy One to be born shall be called the Son of God'" (Luke 1:35). That's how she was going to conceive, so she would remain a virgin and become a mother.

Oh, what a wonderful woman! You know, I kind of imagine, after the angel said that and then told her about Elizabeth conceiving in her old age (saying that Elizabeth was in the six month and nothing would be impossible to God), I think after that, all of Heaven stopped singing. I think every leaf on every tree did not move anymore. I think every flower and every piece of grass stopped growing. I think every bird stopped singing. I think every cow and sheep and everything else in the world kind of just stopped. And there must have been, for a moment, unnoticed by the world a silence that never was before, and never will be again—everybody was holding their breath. Because everything needed to be redeemed—man and creation were waiting to hear what would Mary say. And I would suppose there was a long half-second, because it didn't take her long, but it must have seemed like eternity to those who were waiting. And St. Luke writes, "But Mary said, 'Behold the handmaid of the Lord; be it done to me according to Thy Word'" (Luke 1:38). No hesitation. No question. No lack of trust. No lack of faith. No lack of hope. Only tremendous love. Total absolute belief in the Word of God.

What a woman! Would it not be great if you and I could accomplish the will of God that fast when it comes to a very hard thing, a very difficult thing? And this then became the new Ark of the Covenant, the New Woman. The woman promised in Genesis. At the marriage feast of Cana, the Lord said "woman"—a very unusual thing to say to a mother—because He wanted to let us know who this woman was. And the Father had said to Adam, "I will put enmity between you and the woman" (see Genesis 3:15).

After all these centuries, and with creation deep in sin and darkness, where cruelty was the order of the day and women were nothing—suddenly God raised up a woman to be His Son's Mother. And she said yes. Love her for this, if there is no other reason that you should love her, if Jesus had not given her to us on the Cross and said, "Behold thy Mother," if she had not been declared so holy by the Church, assumed into Heaven, crowned by the Father in the Trinity. She is Mother of Us All, Mediatrix of All Graces, Conceived without Sin, Vessel of Honor, Tower of Ivory — all these wonderous prerogatives of Mary. This is the woman. This wondrous holy masterpiece of God.

> Lord God, I ask that You give us all that special love for Your Son's Mother. Because she is Your masterpiece. Lord Father, when we love her, we glorify Thy mighty power and Thy goodness and Thy miracle of Thy Awesome Word leaping from Thy throne and becoming flesh in our midst through this woman. We thank You for her, Father, and we ask pardon for all those who dislike her, who hate her and spread such lies about her, Lord. We ask Your forgiveness for all those who have never experienced her intercession or her motherly care because of their hatred. We ask, Lord, that You just melt them down and give them the grace to know this wondrous woman whose powerful intercession inspires us, protects us from Your enemy, the world, and the flesh, and leads us to her Son, Jesus. We ask this in Your Holy Name. Amen.

Let us pray the Litany of Our Lady of Loreto:

Holy Mary,
pray for us.
Holy Mother of God,
pray for us.
Holy Virgin of Virgins,
pray for us.
Mother of Christ,
pray for us.

Mother of the Church,
pray for us.
Mother of Divine Grace,
pray for us.
Mother most pure,
pray for us.
Mother most chaste,
pray for us.
Mother inviolate,
pray for us.
Mother undefiled,
pray for us.
Mother most amiable,
pray for us.
Mother most admirable,
pray for us.
Mother of Good Counsel,
pray for us.
Mother of our Creator,
pray for us.
Mother of our Savior,
pray for us.
Mother of mercy,
pray for us.
Virgin most prudent,
pray for us.
Virgin most venerable,
pray for us.
Virgin most renowned,
pray for us.
Virgin most powerful,
pray for us.

A Holy Hour with Mother Angelica

Virgin most merciful,
pray for us.
Virgin most faithful,
pray for us.
Mirror of justice,
pray for us.
Seat of wisdom,
pray for us.
Cause of our joy,
pray for us.
Spiritual vessel,
pray for us.
Vessel of honor,
pray for us.
Singular vessel of devotion,
pray for us.
Mystical Rose,
pray for us.
Tower of David,
pray for us.
Tower of ivory,
pray for us.
House of gold,
pray for us.
Ark of the Covenant,
pray for us.
Gate of Heaven,
pray for us.
Morning star,
pray for us.
Health of the Sick,
pray for us.

"A Marian Holy Hour"

Refuge of sinners,
pray for us.
Comforter of the afflicted,
pray for us.
Help of christians,
pray for us.
Queen of angels,
pray for us.
Queen of patriarchs,
pray for us.
Queen of prophets,
pray for us.
Queen of apostles,
pray for us.
Queen of martyrs,
pray for us.
Queen of confessors,
pray for us.
Queen of virgins,
pray for us.
Queen of all saints,
pray for us.
Queen conceived without original sin,
pray for us.
Queen assumed into Heaven,
pray for us.
Queen of the Holy Rosary,
pray for us.
Queen of families,
pray for us.
Queen of peace,
pray for us.

A Holy Hour with Mother Angelica

Let us pray. Grant, we beseech Thee, O Lord God, that we Thy servants may enjoy perpetual health of mind and body, and by the glorious intercession of the Blessed Mary, ever Virgin, be delivered from present sorrow and enjoy everlasting happiness. Through Christ Our Lord. Amen.

The Magnificat is that wondrous Psalm. It's a canticle, really, that Our Lady said when Elizabeth saw Mary coming to her. This is the wonder of it all. John the Baptist, Elizabeth said, leapt in her womb. Do you know why? Because he was in the presence of his Lord and God, Jesus, Who was in the womb of Mary. Jesus could not have been more than three days old. You see, that's why abortion is so terrible. Jesus already began His act of redemption by sanctifying John. And Elizabeth said, "Blessed art thou among women, and blessed is the fruit of thy womb. And how have I deserved that the Mother of my Lord should come to me?" (Luke 1:41–43). And Jesus was no more than three days old.

And Mary, in her deep humility, said, "My soul magnifies the Lord, and my spirit rejoices in God my Savior; because He has regarded the lowliness of His handmaid; for behold, henceforth, all generations shall call me blessed; because He Who is mighty has done great things for me, and holy is His Name; and His mercy is from generation to generation on those who fear Him. He has shown might with His arm, He has scattered the proud in the conceit of their hearts. He has put down the mighty from their thrones, and has exalted the lowly. He has filled the hungry with good things, and the rich He has sent away empty. He has given help to Israel, His servant, mindful of His mercy—even as He spoke to our fathers—to Abraham and his posterity forever" (Luke 1:46–55).

You see, that's why you have to love Mary. That is why you have to honor her. Why? Because God has done great things for her! And you know by this that Mary was terrific in knowing her Scripture, because some of this comes from Habakkuk, Samuel, Genesis, the Psalms, Sirach, Ezekiel, Job, and Isaiah. She knew her Scripture. She knew who she was, but it was only the power of God that made her who she was. That was the basis of this wondrous woman: her deep, deep humility. She saw herself as that lowly handmaid. And she saw God as that great sculptor in her life—the one who made a lowly maiden into the Mother of His Son.

How can you dislike this woman? It is amazing that we do not look at her in awe, because God has done such great things for her, to her, and with her. It hurts me, and I know it hurts a lot of Catholics too, that we do not quite understand that when we honor this woman, we honor God. I think that people have to understand that in doing so, you do not take a thing away from Jesus. It's like when I went to Rome and I looked at the Sistine Chapel. If Michelangelo were standing next to me and I were to look up at this masterpiece and say, "eh," or make a disparaging remark, it would not only be an insult, it would also show that I do not understand the masterpiece that's up there. And that's how it is with Mary: when you lower her and you speak against her, you are talking about something God created that is a masterpiece. Why are you envious that she was conceived without sin? Why are you envious that she was a virgin after giving birth? What does it matter to you, except that it's a gift to you? These prerogatives of Mary are your gift! Jesus did it for your sake, so He could be born without stain, in the womb of a woman who had no stain of sin. Why is that hard for you? Isn't that wonderful? That God loved you so much that He would do such a great, great thing as to give us Mary—that wondrous woman, the promised, as Our Mother, too? It's wonderful that she was the Mother of Jesus. And now, when I get up in the morning, I know she's also my mother. And she has motherly love and motherly care *just for you.*

God bless you!

Chapter 20

"God's Compassion"

We are going to pray *about* God's compassion, and we are going to pray *for* His compassion, asking the Lord to make us understand the difference between His mercy and our presumption.

Today, we presume upon God's mercy a lot. You ask, what does that mean? Well, it would be presumptuous for you go down the highway in a busy traffic lane at one hundred and twenty miles an hour. That is presumptuous to think that your guardian angel is going to take care of you. That's presumption. It means that you put yourself in great danger saying, "Oh well, the Father will have mercy." You see, it means you use the mercy of God for an excuse to commit sin. That's what presumption does. It uses the mercy of God as an excuse that, at this time, you can commit sin, because He is merciful. That is why it is so horrible before God. So, you cannot just put yourself in occasions of sin and sinful situations and say "Oh well, what's the difference. God has mercy. He is merciful." That is a misuse of a gift of God. And many of us, because we no longer have a sense of sin, a sense of the need to repent and repair for our offenses, we are presumptuous. And that is unfortunate today.

You know, there are tremendous amounts of evil things going on — blasphemous things. Movies, articles, satanic books, just everything that blasphemes the Lord God and His sovereign rights over all mankind. And Christians are so apathetic; we are apathetic because we presume, "Well, somebody else will take care of it," or "God will forgive," or "What's the difference? You can't do anything about it," or even, "The more you yell and scream over it, the more they will go see this movie or that movie, so it's better to be quiet." No! Better to yell and scream and let the Lord God hear you so that you are not responsible! Don't feel sorry for the prophet who seems to be a lone voice in the wilderness. At least he is yelling. At least he is doing something. We can no longer presume on God's mercy. We cannot do that. It's seldom that you see someone who has a sense of sin. It's seldom that you see or hear anyone who has a sense of the necessity to repent and repair for our offenses—repair to God and society. I think the most presumptuous thing is when I hear a person say, "Well, it doesn't matter how much I sin, because Jesus paid for all. He took our sins upon Him, so what's the difference?" Oh, what a terrible state of mind that is. You are responsible for your own sins. You need to say, "I am sorry, Lord." And not only that, but also you need to say that you are sorry for other people who don't say they're sorry.

We call that making reparation not just for your own sins, but for other people's sins as well. And that is because if other people do not make reparation for their sins or are never repentant, then you must do it. St. Paul said that this is a wicked generation. Your lives should redeem it. Well, we know only Jesus redeems us, but St. Paul was talking about that kind of reparation for other people's sins that you and I need to fast and pray over. This country is morally and spiritually dead. We don't want to see anything godly. So you and I must pray, you must pray in your own lives, not just during this Holy Hour, but always pray and ask for God's mercy upon this country, upon the movie industry, the television industry, the newspaper and magazine industry, everything that is in the media that has and does continue to bring such horrid and evil things in your living room and into society.

Lord God, we are as children before Thee. We do not even know when we sin. Give us light. We do not have a sense of horror over Thy name and Thy Presence being blasphemed. We go our way, enjoying Your good things while Your Son is so maligned by the enemy and his cohorts, and we are lethargic. We are apathetic, lazy, afraid, and full of human respect, Lord. We are afraid of repercussions; we are afraid we'll be looked down upon as being ridiculous. We are filled with the fear that paralyzes people and allows the worst of things to happen, because we as Christians do not love You enough to stand tall and fight the good fight. So we ask for forgiveness: forgiveness for our spiritual laziness, and for all of our sins. Lord, we ask You to send Your Spirit upon all Christians in this country, to help us rise up against Your enemy, to rise up and fight the evil by our holiness, compassion, love, peace, joy, and self-control and determination, We pray that we shall be holy, and that we know that we are poor sinners and that we need You, Lord. We are in need of Your mercy.

St. Mark's Gospel 6:30–34 says that "The apostles rejoined Jesus and told Him all they had done and taught." They were sent out two by two. If you remember, they healed the blind, the deaf, those who could not speak, and the paralyzed, and they delivered people from demons. And they taught what Jesus taught them. The Gospel continues: "Then He said, you must come away to some lonely place all by yourselves and rest a while." We live in maybe the busiest age ever. We are so busy that everything has to be instant, because we do not take time to do anything. We do not have time. And yet if you look at it, the thing you have the most of is time. Did you ever realize that? I thought during one of my meditations recently, "Angelica, what are you in a hurry about? You are going to live forever." I mean, I am never going to die. Oh, yes, physically I will, but my soul will not; it is immortal. So are you, so is your soul. What are you rushing around for? You have got all the time in world! You say that you have schedules, you have this or that busy thing. But I do not think that's where we are busy. We are busy in our hearts, we are busy in our minds—that is where we are busy. I do not think we are busy just going from one place to another or doing our work. I think we are so busy with useless thoughts, with hardened hearts, with revenge, with displeasure, with anxiety, with frustration, with worry, with resentment, with guilt, with revenge, with anger. Oh, that is where we are busy. And I think I can prove that by this passage. Because the Lord says, "Let's go out alone and we are going to rest." In other words, "drop it." See, when most of you go to prayer, you don't drop anything—you bring everything with you. This whole load of frustrations and everything, you bring it on your back and you throw it before the Lord. That is great, but why don't you just push it aside after you do that, and just talk to Jesus?

Just love Jesus. You ask, "How do I love Jesus?" You love Him. You might say, "That's an invisible reality." So is your mind. Did you ever see your mind? It's invisible, but it's a reality. Did you ever see how your thought process works? What is it, on a computer? No, it works instantly. Everything you do is because of memory, intellect, and will. It happens so fast you don't know it's happening. You don't see it, but it's real. It's right there. It's real, it's active, it's there all the time. But God is closer to you than breathing and nearer to you than hands and feet. That's pretty near to me. My breathing is pretty near to me. And God is more near than that. He resides in the center, the core of your spirit, your heart, your soul. He lives there. You and He have to go to some lonely place—it doesn't mean you have to go in the desert. You can be in the midst of a crowd and be in a lonely place. Because the lonely place is in your heart.

"God's Compassion"

Our Lord said that when you want to pray to your Father, you should go inside your closet. Not many of you go into your clothes closet and lock the door — you don't do that — because He didn't mean that. He didn't mean that you should go into a dark closet. He meant that your heart is your closet. Your heart is your closet where you can shut the door. It is the lonely place where you can close the door and you and Jesus are alone together. And you need that — Jesus needed it, the apostles needed it, everybody needs it. And you? You say you don't need it? Well you're really in bad shape if you think you don't need that, because obviously you don't know what's going on. Even the Lord Himself asked to be able to draw aside to a lonely place where He could be alone with the Father. It's important to know what He is saying and to do it. Scripture says, "for there were so many coming and going that the apostles had no time even to eat." Have you ever been that busy? I've been that busy. One time I had to eat a small sandwich in the car between places. I mean, that's what you call busy! Going to three or four states in a day is busy. At least it keeps the airlines in business! So there are times in your life where you are going, going, going, going — and yet, I don't think you have to lose sight of this lonely place in your heart. I think that is a cop-out. Because there is nobody between your two ears except you and God, unless you open the door and let the whole world come in and out like a department store — it's then that you have a problem. But while there are times it's like a department store, you can also put out the lights and lock the doors, front and back, and then there is nobody there but you and God. You have to reach that point every day.

So, the apostles and Jesus went out in a boat to a lonely place where they could be by themselves. But the people saw where they were going and they got there ahead of time. How do you like that? Talk about running away. But you know what is so beautiful about this is one sentence here? It's sad, sometimes it looks like it's in the wrong place but it isn't. It says, "As He stepped ashore, He saw a large crowd." They are trying to get away from the crowd because they didn't even have time to eat. It says, "And He took pity on them." Just imagine Jesus in this boat, and as He is getting near the shore, He looks and the whole shoreline is full of people. Just full of people, five or even ten thousand people. And He looks at them and He has such pity. You know why? "Because they were like sheep without a shepherd." I wish this weren't true in our day, but I am afraid it is. Everywhere I go, I find the same crowd. Different faces in different places, but they all look the same. Sheep without a shepherd—that's how they look. Why? Well, they're confused by shepherds, they're confused by teachers, they're confused by leaders. Whether they are political, civil, or religious, because they are told different ways and different things, different goals and different morality. And that's what the Scripture meant, and these people were just as confused then as you are today. You go here and you hear something, you go there and they contradict it, you go somewhere else and you're told something entirely different. That's what being sheep without a shepherd is like, but those of you that are Catholic—you have a Shepherd. You have Jesus the Shepherd. You have the Holy Father, you have the Magisterium, you have your own bishops, but you have shepherds. You need to obey that Chief Shepherd, you need to be obedient to the Chief Shepherd, as we all do. We need to be in union with that Shepherd. Only then do we know for sure that we are on the right path. And we need to understand that. Don't let yourself wander on top of the mountain or in the valley with nobody to look after you. You and I and everyone must be living within the will of God. When you are living within the will of God, you can be sure of His providence, His protections, His mercy, and His compassion. You can be sure of these when you are in His will. When you take yourself out of God's will, you're a lost sheep, so you are subject to wolves. You put yourself in jeopardy. "You go where angels fear to tread."[2] We say that often in funny instances, but it's actually very, very serious. It is a place where God Himself has difficulty protecting you, because you put yourself in occasions of such sin that you are going to fall flat on your face. Now His grace and His light and His compassion and mercy will always follow you to the last moment of your breath, but if you behave in presumptuous ways and you presume upon the mercy of God, you become a stray sheep. Now, I know you are going to quote to me that beautiful passage where the Lord put the ninety-nine away and went after the stray sheep and He took it on His shoulders (Luke 15:4–6). You know why He took it on His shoulders? Because He had to break its legs. That's why He put it around His neck, because in order to keep those sheep from running away again, they broke their legs. By the time they healed, they had learned quickly to stay in one spot. So there comes with it a kind of chastisement, and we bring it upon ourselves.

And so today we see in society many sheep without a shepherd, because we rebel against the Shepherd, we rebel against Jesus, we rebel against His law, we rebel against His gifts. The Eucharist—some of you get so angry when I talk about the Eucharist. Well, if you're going to get angry, now is the time to turn away! Because I am going to say it anyway. The Eucharist is the Body, Blood, Soul, and Divinity of Jesus Christ on earth. And Mary is His Mother. I don't say this to make you angry, I say this to give you light so that you understand what you are giving up and what you are throwing away. You see, we prefer our own ideas, our own way, to the way of God. So we put ourselves outside of His will, and then we are in trouble. In this passage it says, "this is the place where He fed them." That was the first miracle of the loaves and fishes, and we all know what happened. But you see, the apostles were in the will

[2] Alexander Pope, *An Essay on Criticism*, 1711.

of God. They tried to get away to a lonely place, but the crowd followed them. The busyness and the healing and the effort and the counseling and the teaching had to go on. They were dead tired, but they were in the will of God. And with all the demands upon their time, the demands upon their virtue, the demands upon their stamina, the demands upon their strength, and upon their love for Jesus—all those demands, they rose to them as tired as they were, because they were in the will of God. And God performed miracles for them because they were in His will. You can be sure that if you are in the will of God, He will guide and guard you as the apple of His eye. He will protect you as if there were no one else to protect. He will send His angels to guard you lest you dash your foot against a stone. And He will make you bear fruit, because He will bear fruit within you. So it is very important that we seek that lonely place in our hearts. And when it doesn't seem available, and the crowds and the people and everything around us make more and more demands upon us, if we see the will of God, we can be sure of grace and strength and courage and protection and love. We can be sure.

Lord God, we come before You in our nothingness. We beg You to give us the grace to depend entirely upon You, to know Your will, to have enlightened consciences, so that we know what it is You want us to do, Lord. Give us a deeper faith in Your Chief Shepherd, in the Holy Father, in the Magisterium. Give us that faith that moves mountains. Let us know that no matter how hard things are, no matter how difficult, no matter how impossible, You will perform miracles for us as long as we are in Your holy will. For only then can we be sure, Lord, that we know, love, and serve You with open hearts. And if we should stray, as some sheep do often, then bring us back quickly, Lord. Do not let us stray again. Give us what we need to continue our way home. Amen.

"God's Compassion"

Let us pray the Litany of the Most Sacred Heart of Jesus:

Heart of Jesus, Son of the Eternal Father,
have mercy on us.
Heart of Jesus, formed by the Holy Spirit in the womb of
 the Virgin Mother,
have mercy on us.
Heart of Jesus, substantially united to the Word of God,
have mercy on us.
Heart of Jesus, of Infinite Majesty,
have mercy on us.
Heart of Jesus, Sacred Temple of God,
have mercy on us.
Heart of Jesus, Tabernacle of the Most High,
have mercy on us.
Heart of Jesus, House of God and Gate of Heaven,
have mercy on us.
Heart of Jesus, burning furnace of charity,
have mercy on us.
Heart of Jesus, abode of justice and love,
have mercy on us.
Heart of Jesus, full of goodness and love,
have mercy on us.
Heart of Jesus, abyss of all virtues,
have mercy on us.
Heart of Jesus, most worthy of all praise,
have mercy on us.
Heart of Jesus, king and center of all hearts,
have mercy on us.
Heart of Jesus, in whom are all treasures of wisdom
 and knowledge,
have mercy on us.

A Holy Hour with Mother Angelica

Heart of Jesus, in whom dwells the fullness of divinity,
have mercy on us.
Heart of Jesus, in whom the Father was well pleased,
have mercy on us.
Heart of Jesus, of whose fullness we have all received,
have mercy on us.
Heart of Jesus, desire of the everlasting hills,
have mercy on us.
Heart of Jesus, patient and most merciful,
have mercy on us.
Heart of Jesus, enriching all who invoke Thee,
have mercy on us.
Heart of Jesus, fountain of life and holiness,
have mercy on us.
Heart of Jesus, propitiation for our sins,
have mercy on us.
Heart of Jesus, loaded down with opprobrium,
have mercy on us.
Heart of Jesus, bruised for our offenses,
have mercy on us.
Heart of Jesus, obedient to death,
have mercy on us.
Heart of Jesus, pierced with a lance,
have mercy on us.
Heart of Jesus, source of all consolation,
have mercy on us.
Heart of Jesus, our life and resurrection,
have mercy on us.
Heart of Jesus, our peace and our reconciliation,
have mercy on us.
Heart of Jesus, victim for our sins,
have mercy on us.

Heart of Jesus, salvation of those who trust in Thee,
have mercy on us.
Heart of Jesus, hope of those who die in Thee,
have mercy on us.
Heart of Jesus, delight of all the Saints,
have mercy on us.

Jesus, meek and humble of heart,
make our hearts like to Thine.

Let us pray. Almighty and eternal God, look upon the Heart
of Thy most beloved Son and upon the praises and satisfaction which He offers Thee in the name of sinners; and to
those who implore Thy mercy, in Thy great goodness, grant
forgiveness in the name of the same Jesus Christ, Thy Son,
who livest and reignest with Thee forever and ever. Amen.

Psalm 103 is a Psalm on the love of God. It says, "Bless Yahweh,
my soul, bless His Holy Name, all that is in me bless Yahweh, my
soul, and remember all His kindnesses." I want you to see and hear
these verses and then compare them to a life of sin. Compare the
blasphemies that you hear every day, that you see in movies and
books and everything else. Where you are saying, "Bless the Lord,
bless the Lord, my soul," someone else is saying "Hate the Lord,
blaspheme the Lord." And you know, there's only one person that
does that. You must be very careful and make some very, very solid
choices. The Psalmist continues, saying, "What is God? Remember
all of His kindnesses, forgiving all of your offenses, and curing all
your diseases, redeeming your life from the pit, crowning you with
love and tenderness, filling your years with prosperity, and renew-
ing your youth like an eagle's." After all of that, you still want
to blaspheme God? The Psalmist says that Yahweh does what is
right. He is always on the side of the oppressed. "He revealed His

intentions to Moses, His prowess to the sons of Israel, Yahweh is tender and compassionate, slow to anger and most loving." Now, it doesn't say He never gets angry. It says He is "slow to anger." What will be the straw that breaks the camel's back, so to speak? Which blasphemous movie, which final abortion, what will be the final event that makes the Lord say to us "Enough"? It doesn't say that He will not be angry, it says He will be slow to anger. I think we are pushing Him. The Psalm says that His indignation does not last forever; His resentment exists a short time only. Then He *does* get angry, and believe me, God's short time of being angry is long enough for any of us. Remember that. I hope that you and I never experience even the short-term anger of God, because it could wipe us off the face of the earth. And yet sometimes when you see so much evil, you think "Lord, come and save us." He never treats us as our guilt and our sins deserve. The Psalmist is very realistic: "No less than the height of Heaven over earth is the greatness of His love for those who fear Him." To blaspheme God is to have no fear of God. But you know what the Lord said, don't you? Remember: "Do not fear him who destroys the body, and after that, has nothing else he can do. Rather, fear Him who can throw both body and soul into Gehenna" (Matthew 10:28). God takes our sins further away than the East is from the West. Isn't that great? And yet we continue to sin. The Psalmist continues: "As tenderly as the Father treats his children, so Yahweh treats those who fear Him." He knows what we are made of. He remembers we are dust. He says, "Man lasts no longer than grass." Do you have a yard full of grass? Maybe you don't today, because there's a drought. But you last as long as that grass does. "And no longer than a wildflower he lives, one gust of wind and he is gone." All of you that live as if there were no tomorrow. One gust of wind and you're gone, never to be seen again—not in this life, anyway. "Yet Yahweh's love for those who fear Him lasts from all eternity and forever, like

His goodness to their children's children, as long as they keep His covenant and remember to obey His precepts." We have totally taken those two lines out and thrown them to the wind. As a nation we do not keep the covenant with God. We say, "In God we trust." We do not keep that covenant, though, and we do not keep it as a people. The Psalmist continues, "But Yahweh has fixed His throne in Heaven and His empire is over all. Bless God, all you angels. Heroes mighty, you enforce His Word, be attentive to His Words. Bless all His armies and servants to enforce His will. Bless the Lord, O my soul." That is what we should be doing.

That is the call of today: the call of God is for each one of us to become holy, to respond to the needs of our time, and to the needs of God in our time. Think of God first and yourself after that. And remember, He loves you very much, and He deserves your very best.

Chapter 21

"Another Hour of Reparation"

I want to talk about and devote our Holy Hour to making reparation for a film that was released called *The Last Temptation of Christ*.[3]

It is so sad. Not only is it a blasphemous movie, but so many people in the Church and other churches do not perceive the horror of it! That, to me, is the most disheartening aspect. I could halfway understand its popularity among men and women who do not know or believe in Jesus, who could be so hard of heart and have such careless disregard for the faith of a major religion in the world, a faith that they risk destroying. But when I see members of the Church and the press who have not seen the movie — or worse, they have — make glib and trite remarks to the effect that "Christ was only human; it sheds new light on His humanity; it is theologically inert," whatever that means; and other such pablum — it really is unbearable and a cause for great reparation.

Furthermore, that those who do not even know Jesus would purport to make a film about His supposed "last temptation" is just beyond the pale.

So, let us offer another hour of reparation to the Lord God, since I fear that in the eyes of the Eternal Father, this, and other

---

[3] Directed by Martine Scorsese (Universal Pictures, 1988).

movies like it, are the last straw. Imagine! The same Hollywood which built so much of its empire on the strength of films like *Ben Hur: A Tale of the Christ*,[4] remade in 1959,[5] which became the highest-grossing film after *Gone with the Wind*,[6] now making such disgraceful and polar-opposite films!

I beg the Father to glorify His Son and to put an end either to the movie and others like it, or to the world itself. Is it not better that we should be chastised than we should blaspheme? As it says in the Old Testament, "Then David said to Gad, 'I am in great distress; let us fall into the hand of the Lord, for His mercy is great; but let me not fall into the hand of man'" (2 Samuel 24:14, RSVCE). Oh, I am not hopeless or helpless. We shall fight. But this movie, and others like it, being released into movie houses whereby walking in you endanger your immortal soul — this just seems the last straw.

I pray to God the Father to end this scourge.

Lord Father, Your Son came and obeyed Your will. He lived and He died and suffered an ignominious death that has been so maligned and so distorted by this fiction — so distorted as to implant within the minds of men and women and children the seed of blasphemy and irreverence such as has never been known in the history of the world.

Lord Father, I ask forgiveness and mercy. But we need more than that. We need You, Lord Father, to come in our midst by whatever way You wish, and glorify Your Son's name. I ask You to do things to glorify His name, as He has done everything You asked of Him to glorify Your name.

---

[4] Direced by Fred Niblo (Metro-Goldwyn-Mayer, 1925).
[5] Directed by William Wyler (Metro-Goldwyn-Mayer, 1959).
[6] Directed by Victor Fleming (Selznick International Pictures, Metro-Goldwyn-Mayer, 1939).

I ask that You give light to every creature in this country and in the world, and that everyone supporting such films will see their own souls as wicked and evil. I ask, Father, that You manifest your Son in all His glory. I ask, Father, for You to come in glory. I ask, Father, for You to protect the name of Your Son and not let it be blasphemed in such a terrible, terrible way.

And, Lord, I ask and beg You for forgiveness for this country and for the lukewarmness in the Church; for the apathy in the Church; for the lack of knowledge of Thy Son Jesus and the awesomeness of His Majesty.

Though I ask pardon for all our sin, Lord, how can You forgive this sin, when it is blasphemy against Thy Spirit, the work of Your hands? I do ask pardon, Father, for our sins. But I beg you, do not permit this film to degrade your Son, Jesus. Be merciful, but give us what we need to come to our senses — to understand and accept the glory of Your Son. Amen.

St. John says in his first epistle, "Beloved, do not believe every spirit, but test the spirts to see whether they are of God; because many false prophets have gone forth into the world" (1 John 4:1). Well, we tested (that is, we saw) this movie, and it was blasphemous from beginning to end. There are many false prophets in the world, and you can discern the spirits that come from God by this: every spirit which acknowledges that Jesus Christ is the Son of God is *of* God. But the wimp who portrayed Jesus in this blasphemous film is confused, and prays as a child to God that he may become God. You know, it does not take a genius to test the spirit of this movie. It is offered to us very much like when the snake tempted Adam and Eve. (The world is full of snakes; full of wolves in sheep's clothing; full of hirelings, not shepherds. Hirelings have no concern for the sheep.) Think of being offered a piece of rotten meat. It's so rotten that maggots completely cover it and it stinks. Yet, someone says, "Well, you really won't know that you'll get sick to death unless you try it." In other words, "You have to be free to eat this stinking rotten meat. Then you'll know for sure whether you'll be sick." That's what this movie is asking us. They call that plurality. "Give them a chance." That's what the serpent said in the Garden of Eden, though God had said otherwise. "You may freely eat of every tree of the garden; but of the tree of the knowledge of good and evil you shall not eat, for in the day that you eat of it you shall die" (see Genesis 3:3). At the time, Adam and Eve had only experienced goodness.

It's strange isn't it that in these end times, the Lord is permitting the same serpent to administer the same identical test? If you watch that movie, decide for yourself, make your own judgment. But, I say, if you walk into the theater, you are doomed. I say this before God and before you and before every creature in this country and in this world: you are doomed if you walk in the door of a movie house showing such an abominable film. Because just like Eve, who ate that apple, the serpent is going to take you in his tail and gobble you up and you will never have a good, holy, pure thought throughout the rest of your life!

You know, it amazes me that we have become so hardened by sin that blasphemy doesn't even register in our consciences. What a state this world has come to! And now I have much greater understanding when I hear this statement that the Lord made: "Yet when the Son of Man comes, will He find, do you think, faith on earth?" (Luke 18:8). I read the newspapers that said, "Go ahead, see the film. It's not so bad. The blasphemy is not so bad." Yet the very title of the film is blasphemous! How can any man with a crown of thorns on His head, nailed to a tree, having lost most all of His blood, have any lustful thoughts? Are you *out of your mind*? That you can attribute that kind of dream or temptation to the Son of God is *total* blasphemy.

I pray to the Lord Father God that He will rain fire from Heaven if we dare do such a thing. *If we dare do such a thing.* As St. John writes, "He who knows his brother is committing a sin that is not unto death, shall ask, and shall give life to him who does not commit a sin unto death. There is sin until death; I do not mean anyone should ask as to that. All lawlessness is sin, and there is a sin unto death" (1 John 5:16–17). He also writes something very striking in the previous chapter, which I think sums up what we are praying about: "Any spirit that severs Jesus is not of God, but is of antichrist, of whom you have heard that he is coming, and now is already in the world" (1 John 4:3).

I have been told one of the excuses people make for this film is that it is only fiction, the imaginings of a filmmaker. Well, you do not fictionalize the Son of God. All that we should know about the Son of God is given to you in the Gospel. You cannot write a book or a play about pornography and make the Son of God the main actor, and then tell me that you are thereby hoping to increase faith. In the devil, yes! But you cannot increase faith in the Son of God when you tear Him apart and make Him less than a man. And you take away His majesty and His glory and His Divinity and His act of redemption. How far has our human nature gone that we have degraded the Spirit of God, Who has given us a memory, intellect, and will — our very soul? We have degraded our bodies to the animal level, and now we have tried to bring the Son of God down to our animal level. That is the work of Satan. That's the antichrist. Why can't you see that? How in the Lord's name can't Church leaders see that? What kind of leaders urge you to see a movie that will damn your soul? I want to know, what kind of leaders? Hirelings, not shepherds! Hirelings who do not do the work of God!

A Holy Hour with Mother Angelica

I don't know if this is a Holy Hour of reparation or not. I don't know how you make reparations for that. Do you say to God, "I'm sorry" and go your way? Is that what you do? What *do* you do? I guess the only thing we can do now is not only pray, but fight and fight and fight against these evils.

So, I beg of you to say the Rosary, which Our Lady has been asking everybody to say since 1917. I ask you to go to Mass every morning and receive Holy Communion, if possible. And I am asking you to keep saying to Jesus:

I'm sorry, Lord. We have not only grown cold; we have grown evil. We do not even know, Lord, when You are offended anymore. Our hearts are so cold and our faith so weak. Lord, do with this nation and do with this world as You will. We must leave ourselves to Your justice. It is Your justice, Lord God and Father, that I cry out for. It is Your justice, Lord Father, that I ask You to visit upon us. It is Your justice, Lord Father, that I ask for—that You do whatever is necessary to keep Your Son from such blasphemy. I have never prayed to God for justice, for I have always feared it. But now, in the face of this terrible sacrilege, I feel it would be a comfort. Your justice would be a comfort, Lord. For we stand before You a people who no longer know their right hand from their left. We stand before You a people who have lost our way, and though I have confidence in Your mercy, I also have confidence in Your justice. For You are our Father and You chastise those whom You love, that they may come to their senses and adore You, Our Lord God and Father. And, Lord Father, please do not abandon us to ourselves, for that is a punishment we cannot bear. Let us fall into Your hands rather than into the hands of Your enemy. Visit us, Lord, with Your chastisement that we may see the light and no longer offend Thee. Amen.

Lord, have mercy on us.

Christ, have mercy on us.

Lord, have mercy on us.

Christ, hear us.

Christ, graciously hear us.

God, the Father of Heaven,

have mercy on us.

God the Son, Redeemer of the world,

have mercy on us.

God the Holy Spirit,

have mercy on us.

Holy Trinity, One God,

have mercy on us.

Blood of Christ, only-begotten Son of the Eternal
  Father,

save us.

Blood of Christ, Incarnate Word of God,

save us.

Blood of Christ, of the New and Eternal Testament,

save us.

Blood of Christ, falling upon the earth in the Agony,

save us.

Blood of Christ, shed profusely in the Scourging,

save us.

Blood of Christ, flowing forth in the Crowning with
  Thorns,

save us.

Blood of Christ, poured out on the Cross,

save us.

Blood of Christ, price of our salvation,

save us.

A Holy Hour with Mother Angelica

Blood of Christ, without which there is no forgiveness.
save us.
Blood of Christ, Eucharistic drink and refreshment of souls,
save us.
Blood of Christ, stream of mercy,
save us.
Blood of Christ, victor over demons,
save us.
Blood of Christ, courage of Martyrs,
save us.
Blood of Christ, strength of Confessors,
save us.
Blood of Christ, bringing forth Virgins,
save us.
Blood of Christ, help of those in peril,
save us.
Blood of Christ, relief of the burdened,
save us.
Blood of Christ, solace in sorrow,
save us.
Blood of Christ, hope of the penitent,
save us.
Blood of Christ, consolation of the dying,
save us.
Blood of Christ, peace and tenderness of hearts,
save us.
Blood of Christ, pledge of eternal life,
save us.
Blood of Christ, freeing souls from purgatory,
save us.
Blood of Christ, most worthy of all glory and honor,
save us.

Let us pray. Almighty and eternal God, You have appointed Your only-begotten Son the Redeemer of the world, and willed to be appeased by His Blood. Grant we beg of You, that we may worthily adore this price of our salvation, and through its power be safeguarded from the evils of the present life, so that we may rejoice in its fruits forever in Heaven. Through the same Christ our Lord. Amen.

Let us read some beautiful passages from the Old Testament on seeking repentance, including Psalm 51, which is called the Psalm of Repentance:

Have mercy on me, O God, in Your goodness. In Your great tenderness, wipe away my sins. Wash me clean of my guilt, purifying me from my sin. For I am well aware of my faults and I have my sin constantly in mind, having sinned against none other than You, Lord God; having done what You regard as wrong. You are just when You pass sentence on me, blameless when You give judgment. You know I was born guilty, a sinner from the moment of my conception. Yet, since You love sincerity of heart, teach me the secrets of wisdom. Purify me with hyssop until I am clean. Wash me until I am whiter that snow. Instill some joy and gladness into me and let the bones You have crushed rejoice again. Hide Your face from my sins. Wipe out all my guilt. God, create a clean heart in me. Put into me a new and constant spirit. Do not banish me from Your presence. Do not deprive me of Your Holy Spirit. Be my Savior again. Renew my joy, keep my spirit ready and willing. Then I shall teach transgressors their way. To You all sinners will return. Save me from death, God, my Savior, and my tongue will acclaim Your righteousness. Lord, open my lips, and my mouth will speak Your praise. Sacrifice gives You no pleasure;

were I to offer holocausts, You would not have it. My sacrifice is a broken spirit. You will not scorn this crushed and broken heart. Show me favor graciously. Rebuild the walls of Jerusalem. Then there will be proper sacrifice to please You; holocausts and whole oblations and young bulls to be offered on Your altar.

And let us also read Psalm 130, also known as *De Profundis*:

From the depths I called to You, Yahweh. Lord, listen to my cry for help. Listen compassionately to my pleading. If You never overlooked our sins, Yahweh, Lord, could anyone survive? But You do forgive us. For that we revere You. I wait for Yahweh; my soul waits for Him. I rely on His promise and my soul relies on the Lord more than a watchman for the coming of dawn. Let Israel rely on Yahweh as much as the watchman on the dawn. For it is with Yahweh that mercy is to be found, and plenteous redemption. It is He Who redeems us from all our sins.

It was my desire to end this Holy Hour with some kind of hope, but the Psalmist had a broken heart, and so do we, because our Jesus is so maligned and so blasphemed and so degraded to the level of a mad, lustful man. And those who have been chosen by God Himself not only to recognize His Son but to lead others to Him have lost their way. The children are apathetic, they don't care. And so, we say our prayers to God the Father with a broken heart, saying, "Lord, only You can save us. Come, come Lord, defend Your Son."

So often in battle, no matter what kind of battle you fight, there is a sense that at least people understand. I know there are many people out there who *do understand* and they are fighting to the best of their ability, but it seems that there is in this world today, as you read newspapers and listen to programs, a kind of numbness. It exists among those who should be out there, leading people of every denomination; there seems to be an indifference; there seems to be an inability to understand this battle, this fight.

Maybe we need to define blasphemy. Maybe that's our problem. We don't even know what it is. I know one minister said, as reported in the paper, that he didn't even know what the word meant, nor could he spell it. Well, I'm not asking you to spell it. But maybe we need to define it. The film, which has been the subject of our Hour of repentance, is just wholesale blasphemy from beginning to end. There is nothing that can be done to redeem it. No editing can fix it. The degradation and annihilation of faith is at its core. That is why I call it the work of the antichrist. And it is part of the antichrist movement that has given this film its power to overcome your mind, your memory, your imagination, your intellect, your will, and to destroy them—to destroy faith totally, especially the faith of teenagers who are not yet formed. Society seems perfectly content to let this thing go forward, which, in this day and age, is unbelievable. It is why, as I say, I feel it is the last straw. People are perfectly content to let them try and bring Jesus, the Son of God, down to the level of a sinful, lustful man, and that gives everybody the ability to set Him aside totally and to accept a new Christ—an antichrist.

Please be careful. We are *not* dealing with just a *movie*. It's a *movement* we are dealing with—two battles for your soul. This is not child's play. You deal with the fire below or the anger of God above. Our hope is that we stand tall and we fight for Jesus, that we uphold His name, His honor, and His glory.

Blessed forever be the name of Jesus, the Only Son of God!

Chapter 22

"Our Lady's Special Appeal for Repentance"

This Holy Hour is one of reparation, especially viewed through the prism of Our Lady's special appeal in this regard. It concerns the need to ask the Lord to know what it takes turn our lives over to Him — to say, "Jesus, You're the only Way, the Truth, and the Life."

We will also focus on the need to ask Our Lady for special help, especially for those whose lives are so unhappy and so miserable. Perhaps their married and family lives are in shambles. Our Lady keeps telling us over and over to pray. She's talking to people all over the world — to say yes to God, and to begin to follow the commandments and precepts of the Church, and to ask for forgiveness and mercy. Our Lady of Fatima wants to come closer to our hearts. It seems she wants to reach out and touch us all, rather than touch just one person here or one person there, but to touch countless souls across the globe. Her heart is reaching out in a very pleading and motherly way for us to repent.

There is a great need for families to pray and to become reconciled with God on the way to family harmony.

Let us pray the Litany of Our Lady of Loreto:

Holy Mary,
pray for us.

A Holy Hour with Mother Angelica

Holy Mother of God,
pray for us.
Holy Virgin of Virgins,
pray for us.
Mother of Christ,
pray for us.
Mother of the Church,
pray for us.
Mother of Divine Grace,
pray for us.
Mother most pure,
pray for us.
Mother most chaste,
pray for us.
Mother inviolate,
pray for us.
Mother undefiled,
pray for us.
Mother most amiable,
pray for us.
Mother most admirable,
pray for us.
Mother of Good Counsel,
pray for us.
Mother of our Creator,
pray for us.
Mother of our Savior,
pray for us.
Mother of mercy,
pray for us.
Virgin most prudent,
pray for us.

Virgin most venerable,
pray for us.
Virgin most renowned,
pray for us.
Virgin most powerful,
pray for us.
Virgin most merciful,
pray for us.
Virgin most faithful,
pray for us.
Mirror of justice,
pray for us.
Seat of wisdom,
pray for us.
Cause of our joy,
pray for us.
Spiritual vessel,
pray for us.
Vessel of honor,
pray for us.
Singular vessel of devotion,
pray for us.
Mystical Rose,
pray for us.
Tower of David,
pray for us.
Tower of ivory,
pray for us.
House of gold,
pray for us.
Ark of the Covenant,
pray for us.

A Holy Hour with Mother Angelica

Gate of Heaven,
pray for us.
Morning star,
pray for us.
Health of the Sick,
pray for us.
Refuge of sinners,
pray for us.
Comforter of the afflicted,
pray for us.
Help of christians,
pray for us.
Queen of angels,
pray for us.
Queen of patriarchs,
pray for us.
Queen of prophets,
pray for us.
Queen of apostles,
pray for us.
Queen of martyrs,
pray for us.
Queen of confessors,
pray for us.
Queen of virgins,
pray for us.
Queen of all saints,
pray for us.
Queen conceived without original sin,
pray for us.
Queen assumed into Heaven,
pray for us.

Queen of the Holy Rosary,
pray for us.
Queen of families,
pray for us.
Queen of peace,
pray for us.

Let us pray. Grant, we beseech Thee, O Lord God, that we Thy servants may enjoy perpetual health of mind and body, and by the glorious intercession of the Blessed Mary, ever Virgin, be delivered from present sorrow and enjoy everlasting happiness. Through Christ Our Lord. Amen.

Chapter 23

"Being a Disciple of Jesus"

Let's talk about discipleship, and what it means to follow Jesus. We need to follow Jesus in every aspect of His life.

You know, people often wonder why Jesus was baptized. He had no Original Sin. He had nothing to atone for. He was baptized to give us the Sacrament of Baptism, to sanctify the water and to give us an example. There are not many examples of repentance today, though, because not many people think they need to repent.

So during this Holy Hour, we need to ask the Lord to forgive us our many, many sins, failings, and imperfections.

A lot of people think, "Well, I don't do any big sins." Well, you know, you can get a full gallon of water all at one time, or you can fill a gallon slowly, drop by drop. One time, we had a spigot that leaked and so I put a little basin under it. I was surprised that in the morning, the basin was completely full. It hadn't looked like it was dripping that much.

Now let's imagine that that those little drops are what we would call venial sins, or imperfections, frailties, and weaknesses. They keep going. They don't stop. The next thing you know, your bowl is full. When we ignore these little lies, these little instances of a lack of charity, these little instances of gossip or whatever else that we do constantly—offending our neighbor, rashly judging our neighbor, condemning our neighbor—just a thousand things that we do every day, they pile up. And the next thing you know, you have a gallon jug full of those little water drops.

There are two remedies for that. One is the remedy of the Eucharist, and the other is the remedy of Confession. Every time you receive Communion with a contrite heart, a humble heart, and you have gone to Confession—you can go to Communion every morning; oh, what a wonderful thing—not only does it nourish you with the Body, Blood, Soul, and Divinity of Jesus, but it gives you new life. It gives you eternity. It gives you salvation. It gives you everything you need. And it forgives all those drops one at a time, those little drops which we call venial sin. It forgives them.

You have say to the Lord when you go to Communion, "Lord, I want this Precious Body and Blood, Soul and Divinity that I am taking within myself to clean out my heart of all these little things that I do. Most the time, I don't even know I'm doing them." It just happens so quickly. Your mother wants you do something, and you say no. And, then you repent and go back. A little laziness here. A little laziness there. We don't have a contrite heart. We don't have a conscience anymore that is sensitive or scrupulous. Today, we either bury our conscience, or we become overly scrupulous. But that middle road that makes me sensitive to hurting my parents or hurting my brothers and sisters and my neighbor—it should make me sensitive, not overly scrupulous, but sensitive. It should make me think, "Oh, I did something I shouldn't have done, and I'm very, very sorry." Then I should go to Confession, the marvelous Sacrament of Reconciliation.

Now, a lot of you don't go to Communion, and you are dusty. That's another comparison. For example, if you had a beautiful table and it was dusty, it doesn't take much to wipe it off and make it look beautiful again. But if you had a whole clod of mud on it, or acid, or anything damaging, now that is a job. That's exactly like mortal sin. And the more that you commit mortal sin, grievous sin, the more acid you are putting on this beautiful table. That takes a lot of work to repair. You have to do a re-finishing job. It's not like dust that you just wipe off.

Now, the Sacrament of Reconciliation does both small and large repairs. It prepares you for discipleship. You can't follow Jesus if you do not try to be like Him. To be a disciple today is to be someone who follows and wants to be like Jesus. How can we do that if we're not even conscious of our condition as sinners? We will not acknowledge our condition as sinners, and as a consequence of this, we won't even ask for forgiveness. You see, that's how bad it is today.

And, so, what I would like to do is to make you aware — not scrupulously aware, but aware — that we are all sinners. I am a sinner. Everybody here is a sinner, every day. We're impatient, we're not tolerant, we speak before we think. It's larger things, as well as a lot of little things. It's that dust on the table. We need to say, "Jesus, I am heartily sorry for my sins, for all these little things that I do all day long that offend You and that offend my neighbor." I offend my neighbor, I offend God. Jesus said, "Amen I say to you, as long as you did not do it for one of these, the least of My brethren, you did not do it for Me" (Matthew 25:45) You say, "I'm not doing it." Yeah, you do it a lot. But one Communion can wipe it away, just like a dust cloth takes away all the dust and that table looks beautiful again. Some of you who have acid spots and burn spots and mud and old food that dropped on your table — that table looks horrible — you need more than a dust cloth. You're going to need a conversion experience. You must say, "Yes, I am a sinner. Yes, I have done these things. Yes, I am sorry." And then, put the axe to the root. What does that mean? It means that you really want to conquer that fault — *really want to conquer* that sin, that grievous sin.

So ask the Lord tonight, especially before you retire, ask the Lord to give you the grace of repentance. Sometimes, we have to ask the

Lord for things that we should have — things that should be part and parcel of our very being. I'll bet that if you don't ask for forgiveness from God, you also don't ask for forgiveness from your neighbor. If you are not repentant to the Lord, if you don't say, "Lord, I am sorry," I'll make a bet that you never say you're sorry to your neighbor.

How many marriages have broken up because you consistently offend each other and you never say before you go to bed that you're sorry? "Do not let the sun set on your anger!" (see Ephesians 4:26). Well, many suns and many moons have set on your anger, and so there is not a sense that we are all sinners, that we all need repentance, we all need to repair and to become better than we are. The reason we don't admit this is because the world's positive thinkers, all these New Agers, they keep building us up. They say, "You're a deity. You're wonderful. You're okay. You're beautiful and you can do anything you want." That's a lot of hogwash. We're poor sinners and we have a hard time being good, and without God's grace, without Jesus, we cannot be good. Don't let anybody tell you about another Messiah. There is no other Messiah. There are not one hundred different versions of Jesus. There is only one Jesus, one Savior, one Lord, one King, one God. There is no one else. Everything else is a lie. And you buy lies, because you can't see the truth in yourself, and you don't see the truth in anybody else. So, we buy lies. We buy them consistently. So, my friends, let us ask the Lord to show us ourselves and to repent.

Let us pray.

Lord God, give us the grace to know Thee, to know ourselves, to love Thee, to love ourselves, to do to my neighbor what I want done to myself. Give me a deep awareness of my life, my faults, my weaknesses — in a deep humility — so that I might just give them all to You, Lord Father, and put them all in Your Holy Sacred Heart. Amen.

"Now after six days," St. Mark writes, "Jesus took Peter, James and John, and led them up to a high mountain off by themselves" (Mark 9:2). Now, you know that was a cause of great jealousy among the brethren, because for some unknown reason, at least unknown to them, Jesus was seemingly always taking these three apart and most especially John. These three and Jesus would do things together and see His miracles that the others did not see. So here in the Gospel they are going up a mountain by themselves, and it caused a lot of jealousy among the other disciples. What amazes me is that the Lord never stopped doing it. He didn't say "Oh, I'm causing a lot jealousy, I'd better back up a little bit." He said nothing of the sort. He would just ask the others every so often, "What were you talking about on the way?" As a result, He would get the jealousy out of them. But He wasn't about to change what He was doing. Why not? Because these three men had special missions from God. He loved them and He loved the other apostles.

You can really only love in one way, and that's in an infinite way. Peter was the leader; he was Vicar of Christ. James was the first apostle to be martyred, and John was the mystic. John, especially, had three different missions: He is typically depicted as an eagle. John was going to take care of Jesus' Mother after His death; he was going to be with the Church the longest (he died around 102 A.D.); and this is the man that gave us the marvelous book of Revelation, the book of St. John, the Epistle of St. John. They're fiery books, and they are filled with the Divinity of Jesus.

It was absolutely necessary that the faith of these three men be grounded and deep, because they had things to do that the other apostles did not have to do. Here we are given a great blessing on how futile it is to rashly judge, to try to interpret on our own. We might think, "God loves this one more than that one, or this one has the hotline to Heaven." This is all foolishness. People may pray a lot and appear united to the Lord, but that does not take anything away from you. You have not only the capability, but you have also been given by God all of the graces you need to be as great in holiness as these apostles. We just don't make the effort.

So, He took them up a high mountain and in St. Mark's Gospel it says that there in their presence, He "was transfigured before them" (see 9:2). Well, that must have been a shock. You know, I sometimes feel sorry for the apostles because they got one shock after another. Nobody gets transfigured in their lifetime or any lifetime that they know of, but here they are standing atop this mountain, and all of a sudden, Jesus begins to change. St. Mark writes, "And His garments became shining, exceedingly white as snow, as no fuller on earth can whiten" (9:3). Suddenly His garment was like light itself! And the three apostles looked at that and had no idea what was going on. "And there appeared to them Elias (Elijah) with Moses" (9:4). Here they see the prophet who was taken up in a chariot, and Moses, the giver of the law, who walked with God, talked to God, and was so holy, and with a face so radiant that people could not look at it. He had to put a veil on his face when he came down from Mount Sinai. Well, here they are—Moses and Elijah. Those poor apostles didn't know what to do! Elijah and Moses "were talking with Jesus" (9:4). We wonder what their conversation was about. I would imagine that the Lord was talking to them about the coming redemption. This redemption began at the Incarnation, but the final stages of this redemption were to be all that He would suffer. These men were prophets, but I don't think what they wrote was anywhere near what was being revealed to them. And Jesus was talking to Moses because Moses' part of salvation history was about to end, and something very new was coming. And Elijah, I think, was told, because he's going to come back again, this is what he is working towards and what one day he will have to defend.

And, so the Lord is talking to both of them and they're both in that limbo. Both are about to be released so they can see the face of the Father that they spoke to and loved, and it was they through whom the Father spoke to the people of God. He wanted to explain that, now, the Messiah was here and that things would be totally changed.

Well poor Peter! You know, Peter was such a wonderful man. I love him because he is very much like I am. We both think after we talk. That's when you bite your tongue and say, "Oh, why'd I have to say that?"

So Peter said, "Rabbi, it is good for us to be here. And let us set up three tents, one for Thee, one for Moses, and one for Elias [Elijah]" (9:5).

I mean Peter was just amazed. Who would ever think he would have ever seen Moses! All those doctors of law scratching their heads, trying to figure out what Moses meant here, what he meant there. And now Peter is looking right at him and Elijah. So, what does he say? "It is good for us to be here." Isn't that true of all of us? We get a little consolation and we think we've got it made. When I was a novice, which seems like centuries ago, every day, almost, I would come up with a new secret, a new idea, through which I could really keep close to the Lord this week. And every time it worked. And, I'd think, "I got it! From now on, it's going to be smooth sailing." Now you see, I forgot about the subject matter that Jesus was talking to Moses and Elijah about: the Cross. And every time you think you've got it made, you think, "Lord, let's just stay here." No matter how miserable you are in this world, you don't think of Heaven. Nobody talks about Heaven. Nobody talks about dying. It's a hush-hush subject. But we're all going to die. And you know, if we want to stay here, sometimes as miserable as that is, we wouldn't want to go; we think it's good here. We think, "Let's stay here. Just make it comfortable for me here. I'll pray to You, Jesus, once in a while, open this little box on Sunday; and then push it back in. I'll render thanks and praise and honor and glory to You. Just let me stay here." That's exactly what Peter is saying. He's saying, "Isn't it wonderful? Let's make three tents—one for you, one for Moses, one for Elijah." He means, "Let's not begin a new religion. Look how nice this is! You know, we can just build three tents. I'll run down and tell all the doctors of the law and the Scribes and the Pharisees and the people to come up here, and they'll see You and then everything will be fine. We're just going to put the whole thing together. We're going to have the Old Testament and we're going to have the New Testament, and it's all going to be great. Just great. I mean, why do we have to destroy one to have another one?"

Well it says in the Gospel, "For he did not know what to say, for they were struck with fear" (9:6).

Do you ever get in that position where you say something very stupid because you do not know what to say? And it isn't always an embarrassing situation. You meet somebody new and you can say the dumbest thing. And afterwards, it's over. You think, why did I say that stupid thing? Well, that's exactly what Peter did. St. Mark writes that Peter did not know what to say, and they were fearful and didn't want to explain it. When you don't understand the mysteries of God, maybe that's what you do; you think, "Oh, we'll just leave it go and forget about it. I mean, why delve into it? Why defend against a blasphemous movie? Why do we have to make waves? Why do we have talk about sin and repentance and reparation and all these disagreeable subjects? Why don't we just let it go? It'll pass. We'll make three tents. One tent for the wicked, another tent for the lukewarm, and one tent for the good. They all live together. Let it go. Let it ride." They were scared, that's all. We're still running scared, too; we're still doing stupid things. We don't want to make waves. We don't want to warn people of the chastisement that is coming. We don't want to say that the Lord is going to purify His world and make it new and beautiful and wonderful again. We don't want to hear that. We just want to be our miserable selves on top of our little mountains and make those three tents—we do not want to change, we do not want a mansion.

St. Mark continues: "And there came a cloud overshadowing them, and there came a voice out of the cloud saying, 'This is My beloved Son; hear Him'" (9:7).

Now, this is real confirmation that *this is the Son of God*. Even God knew that these men, in order to follow Jesus unto death, had to have confirmation. That's okay. We have to have confirmation of signs and warnings. That's why Our Lady appeared at Fatima, for example, along with the other apparitions of Our Lady—we need confirmation. God the Father confirmed for us that this is His Son. And what does He say? "Listen to Him."

Do you listen to Jesus? Do you listen to the Bible? Or do you listen to these newfangled theologians and psychologists and psychiatrists and newspapermen and editorials and news programs? Is that your gospel? It's not going to hold water when the earth shakes. And when the earth begins to tremble under our feet, I can tell you one thing: none of them are going to be there. None of them will be there to help us. Only God will. We're going to have to go to Jesus and we're going to have to listen to Him because His voice is going to boom throughout the world. And then we are going to do exactly what it says here: the disciples, frightened as they were, hid their faces, "and suddenly looking round, they no longer saw anyone with them but only Jesus" (9:8).

That's the beauty of purification.

Now, we see everything. We see greed, ambition, lust, drunkenness, immorality. We see all of that. That's all we see. That's all we hear. That's all we know. That's all we want. But when the cloud comes and overshadows us, we will look and see no one else—only Jesus.

A Holy Hour with Mother Angelica

Lord God, we have sinned against Thee and we are sorry. Forgive us our sins. Forgive us and let Thy mercy still penetrate our hearts. And if it is Thy will that Thou purify us, Lord God, then let us be strong and let us look up and see no one but Jesus, for Jesus is our hope. In Jesus is our strength. In Jesus is everything we need — to know, to love, and serve Him with Mary as our Intercessor. Amen.

Let us pray the Litany of the Holy Cross:

Holy Cross, where on the Lamb of God was offered,
save us, O Holy Cross.
Hope of Christians,
save us, O Holy Cross.
Pledge of the resurrection of the dead,
save us, O Holy Cross.
Shelter of persecuted innocents,
save us, O Holy Cross.
Guide of the blind,
save us, O Holy Cross.
Way of those who have gone astray,
save us, O Holy Cross.
Consolation of the poor,
save us, O Holy Cross.
Restraint of the powerful,
save us, O Holy Cross.
Destruction of the proud,
save us, O Holy Cross.
Trophy of victory over Hell,
save us, O Holy Cross.
Terror of demons,
save us, O Holy Cross.

Hope of the hopeless,
save us, O Holy Cross.
Father of orphans,
save us, O Holy Cross.
Defense of widows,
save us, O Holy Cross.
Counsel of the just,
save us, O Holy Cross.
Judge of the wicked,
save us, O Holy Cross.
Safeguard of childhood,
save us, O Holy Cross.
Strength of manhood,
save us, O Holy Cross.
Last hope of the aged,
save us, O Holy Cross.
Light of those who sit in darkness,
save us, O Holy Cross.
Liberty of slaves,
save us, O Holy Cross.
Preached by apostles,
save us, O Holy Cross.
Glory of martyrs,
save us, O Holy Cross.
Chastity of virgins,
save us, O Holy Cross.
Joy of priests,
save us, O Holy Cross.
Foundation of the Church,
save us, O Holy Cross.
Salvation of the world,
save us, O Holy Cross.

Destruction of idolatry,
save us, O Holy Cross.
Condemnation of the ungodly,
save us, O Holy Cross.
Support of the weak,
save us, O Holy Cross.
Medicine of the sick,
save us, O Holy Cross.
Strength of the paralytic,
save us, O Holy Cross.
Bread of the hungry,
save us, O Holy Cross.
Fountain of those who thirst,
save us, O Holy Cross.
Clothing of the naked,
save us, O Holy Cross.
Lamb of God, Who takes away the sins of the world,
spare us, O Lord.
Lamb of God, Who takes away the sins of the world,
graciously hear us, O Lord.
Lamb of God, Who takes away the sins of the world,
have mercy on us.
Christ, hear us.
Christ, graciously hear us.

Let us pray. O God, Who for the redemption of the world
were pleased to be born in a stable and to die upon a Cross,
O Lord, Jesus Christ, by Thy holy sufferings which we, Thy
unworthy servants, call to mind by Thy Holy Cross and by
Thy death, deliver us from the pains of Hell and vouchsafe
to conduct us as Thou didst conduct the good thief who

was crucified with Thee, Who lives and reigns in the unity of the Father and the Holy Spirit, forever and ever. Amen.

Psalm 90 is a Psalm through which we can look at God, face ourselves, and depend upon Him.

Lord, Thou hast been our dwelling place in all generations.

Before the mountains were brought forth, or ever Thou hadst formed the earth and the world from everlasting to everlasting, Thou art God.

Thou turnest man back to the dust and sayest, 'Turn back, O children of men!' For a thousand years in Thy sight are but as yesterday when it is past, or as a watch.

Thou dost sweep men away; they are like a dream, like grass which is renewed in the morning; in the morning it flourishes and is renewed; in the evening it fades and withers.

For we are consumed by Thy anger; by Thy wrath we are overwhelmed. Thou hast set our iniquities before Thee, our secret sins in the light of Thy countenance.

For all our days pass away under Thy wrath, our years come to an end like a sigh. The years of our life are three-score and ten, or even by reason of strength fourscore; yet their span is but toil and trouble; they are soon gone, and we fly away.

Who considered the power of Thy anger, and Thy wrath according to the fear of Thee? So teach us to number our days that we may get a heart of wisdom.

Return, O Lord! How long? Have pity on Thy servants! Satisfy us in the morning with Thy steadfast love, that we may rejoice and be glad all our days. Make us glad as many days as Thou hast afflicted us, and as many years as we have seen evil. Let Thy work be manifest to Thy servants, and Thy glorious power to their children. Let the favor of the Lord Our God be upon us, yea, the work of our hands establish Thou it.

You know, you can meditate on this Psalm for a whole evening. Our lives last seventy years, eighty if you're in good health. Some of you are nearing the end of the hill. But they all add up to anxiety and trouble, isn't that true? Over in a trice and then we're gone, just like that. Who yet has felt the full force of God's fury? Oh, we're going to do that pretty soon. Who has learned to fear the violence of God's rage? We don't know what God's rage is. We are children of mercy. We are children of the New Covenant. We are children of redemption. Teach us to count how few days we have, the Psalmist says. I think that takes on a special meaning now. How much longer do we have? Personally, I don't think we have much longer. Now, don't get excited. You're not going to be blown to bits, but just shaken up a little bit. So, you can do exactly what it says here: "Gain wisdom of heart." Let us wake in the morning filled with God's love, and let us sing and be happy all our days. He will make our future as happy as our past was sad. That's what's going to happen! May the sweetness of the Lord be upon us. May everything we do succeed.

If you want a humble thought, this is a great Psalm to read, perhaps to help dissipate the anger which burns us up, and help us understand God's fury—God having summed up our sins and knowing all our secrets and those little skeletons in the closet. You may have forgotten them, but He never forgets them. Our days dwindle under Your wrath, the Psalmist says. Our lives are over like a breath, in a snap. That fast!

So, when you read this Psalm, you get your act together a little bit, because there is justice, there is mercy, there is love, there is compassion, there are all these beautiful things in God. But there are often times when we have to pull ourselves together, and if we don't, *God does it for us.* And the Lord pleads with us, He challenges us, He does it through the Church, He does it by signs of all kinds. And I guess we either don't want to see signs, or we're frightened and we think the most horrible thing is happening. We don't think of God's infinite love bringing us to a greater, a better, a newer life.

Presumption is when you presume upon God's mercy while doing nothing to align yourself with His will. In other words, the feeling of "I can do anything I want. God doesn't see. God doesn't care." Or, you're the one who waits until you're very old to straighten up. In the meantime, you are going to sow your wild oats and do the best you can and get as much pleasure out of life as you can. Well, that's presumption. You cannot presume that you are going to live even another twenty-four hours. People die in accidents. People die sudden deaths. All kinds of things can happen. So that's presumptuous to put off or to presume on God's mercy. You think, "Well I can commit the sin now because God understands," or you say "He's a loving Father and doesn't care if I have an adulterous affair or if I get drunk." Yes, He does care. Putting yourself in a position of presumption goes along with being lukewarm. If you are lukewarm, nine times out of ten you are going to be presumptuous. You don't want to take any chances today.

I want you to say the Rosary. I want you to say it as many times a day as you can. At least say it once. It's five decades: that's fifty Hail Marys, five Our Fathers, plus three more Hail Marys at the beginning, another Our Father, and the Creed. The Rosary is a powerful weapon. We could do away with the whole chastisement if we said this Rosary. So, if you get scared or you have anxieties and frustration and your family is falling apart, and you're falling apart, and everybody is falling apart—this is the way to keep it going all together. It's an unbroken chain, and a link with God. Use it!

Chapter 24

"The Passion of Christ, Prophesied"

We're going to talk about Jesus and Mary, as always, and we're also going to talk about the prophecy of the Passion of Jesus.

One reason why we can have such a hard time being repentant is because we do not remember the Passion. It doesn't seem to be the "in" thing to do. You very seldom hear any sermon or anything in a prayer book that will encourage you to concentrate on, meditate upon, or contemplate on the Passion of Jesus. We are so drawn to the exultation of self today that we try to do everything we can—sometimes even in our prayer lives—to exalt ourselves; to make ourselves feel good; to make ourselves feel assured; to make ourselves feel like we're making progress. So we put ourselves in a specific category of prayer or spiritual life: we want proof. We want to see what God is doing in our lives. We want fruit. We want assurance.

It just seems like we are running around in circles when we do that, because Jesus emptied Himself, as St. Paul tells us. He emptied Himself and He did not cling to His Divinity. He came down to our level. The essence of our redemption is love through suffering—love through pain; love through humiliation. I do not understand how we can think *even for a moment* that we're going to get straight to Heaven in some static state, and that all we need is to *feel* holy. Jesus was the Son of God—He *is* the Son of God—and yet He suffered so much that I cannot even fathom the amount of suffering that was heaped upon the Lord. The humiliation of becoming man would certainly be enough. Sometimes, because we are all so proud, we think, "Hey that's not a humiliation." Well, if we understood *anything* about the Divinity of Jesus, we would know it was a great humiliation; it was a great act of love. It was the greatest humiliation and act of love. I wonder if sometimes that's one reason why we cannot even feel any type of sorrow for our sins. If you do not know the Man of Sorrows, then how are you going to understand the sorrows of Jesus, the sorrows of Mary, and what it took to redeem you?

There are people who will take the opposite view. "He had to do it," they say. Oh, that's very bad. He didn't have to do anything, and neither did Mary. They did it out of love. You have a God who wants to love you. You have a God that loves you and you have a God who wants you to love Him back. That's why you were created. So, when you muddy up this image of Jesus, of the Trinity, it takes forgiveness, confession, absolution, and deep repentance to get rid of that mud in your soul—that muddiness. You know that you can't see your reflection in a muddy pond. We have a little pond out here with some fish in it. Sometimes it looks green and sometimes it looks brown and muddy. And, no one could lean over and see their reflection in it, because it's just so muddy and has too many other things in there. Well, that's exactly the way it is with our souls. Sin muddies the waters. Sin covers us with a shadow, and it's not the Spirit's shadow. Sin covers us with mud. It covers us with grease. It covers us with acid. And so the image of Jesus is marred, or sometimes the image of Jesus isn't there at all. We call that mortal sin, meaning grievous sin, when we deliberately do something to offend God.

Just like rubbing off a little spot here and there and we see a little gray area that never gets white. It never gets clean. We never get the light to shine through. So it is necessary for us to take a look at Jesus and say, "This is what my sins did. *This is what my sins did.* He died for me. He was crucified for me. He was beaten up for me. He was crowned with thorns for me." We need to say, "I'm sorry, Lord. I'm sorry for my sins. I'm sorry. I am so stubborn and proud and arrogant and insensitive and selfish and jealous and ambitious and caustic. I'm sorry Lord. I'm gossipy. I'm all of these things, but I'm sorry. I ask You to wipe me clean. I put myself under Your Cross. I put myself under Your Precious Blood."

> Lord God, give us a repentant heart that we may be sensitive to the things that offend Thee; that we may be sensitive to sin; that we may be sensitive, Lord. Not scrupulous, but sensitive. Give us light that we may be aware when we are in danger of occasions of sin. Give us that sensitivity so we can be really and truly sorry for all our sins. Amen.

In St. Mark's Gospel, we have the second prophecy of the Passion when it says, "And leaving that place, they were passing through Galilee, and He did not want anyone to know it" (9:30). He wanted some time alone with His disciples. The disciples were going to build His Church, and they had to know deeper things. They had to have more faith and hope and love, and He needed time with them. He did not want people to know He was there, and He was telling the disciples something very important, something that the crowds would never have understood. St. Mark writes, "'The Son of Man is to be betrayed into the hands of men, and they will kill him; and having been killed He will rise again on the third day.' But they did not understand the saying and were afraid to ask Him" (9:31–32).

You know, we don't like prophecies. We do not like woeful prophecies, we don't like prophecies that are telling us really painful things. We react the same way today as they did then. We just don't want to hear. But Jesus wanted the apostles to know. Why? Because if they knew ahead of time, they would be ready, they would not be tempted or tested. That's why in the Garden, He said, "Watch and pray, that you may not enter into temptation" (Matthew 26:41). That you may not be put to the test." What was the test? It was whether their faith would waver. That was the test. Would their faith in Jesus waver? They didn't pray, though, and it wavered. It wavered, and they fled. They denied Him. Only one, the one who loved Him deeply, followed Him and took care of His Mother. Only one out of twelve.

The apostles were being told, "Look, this is the world. It cannot go on like this; the Lord is going to purify it so that we will have a beautiful world, a wonderful world, again. Just like Jesus is saying that you cannot be redeemed unless you go through this. We have to go through this—whatever it is—so that we would have a world that was created by God, a world that is filled with love and peace and joy; filled with the power of the Spirit, not the power of Satan. So He said, "The Son of Man is to be betrayed." Nobody wants to hear that. Do you love someone deeply? You don't want them to say, "Well, I'm not going to make it very long. I won't be with you. Why? Because somebody is going to put me to death." You would be petrified, too.

But, He said that He would rise from the dead three days later. Isn't that wonderful? What hope that gives us! They never heard the last part. Because if they had heard it and believed it, had they prayed and pondered it like Our Lady did, they would have known about this Crucifixion. They would have walked with Jesus and prayed with Him and prayed for Him, and they would have prayed for Our Lady and for themselves. They would have had the strength to continue walking the Way of the Cross.

But they didn't pray just like you and I are now not praying. He showed them a sign. This is going to happen. And we don't see signs either; we don't see warnings. Yet, they are all around us—floods, earthquakes, hurricanes, tornadoes. You say, "Oh, we'll always have them." Oh, not the way we're having them now! See, and understand. Just as there was this necessity of having this great upheaval so that we could be redeemed and have a new world a new religion a new church, a spirit within them. All these wonderful things: the New Testament, the knowledge about the life of Jesus, the Eucharist, Our Lady, the saints, the angels—everything would have been unknown to us, unapproachable, had He not redeemed us, had they not had to go through this terrible purification. And it is no different today. We have strayed as if there were no Jesus. We have strayed as if there were no redemption. So, He has no choice. But, it's only so that we have a new world, a new earth, a new spirit, a new attitude, a new love, real love for your neighbor, and safety, goodness, love, and kindness.

The apostles did not understand what He said, and they were afraid to ask. Don't be afraid to ask! Say to the Lord, "Lord, what's coming? Prepare my heart. Am I ready? Is my soul in tune with Yours? I want a world where You are honored and glorified and praised. I want a world that's safe for children, and where there's no abortion or murder or lying or cheating. I want a world that's not filled with all the evil that this world is so filled with, including real hatred—nation for nation; family for family; brother for sister; parents for children; children for parents. I want a world that's a family. I want a world that's good and where the air is clean, and where people love You, Lord." You say, "Well, you're asking for Heaven!" No, I'm only asking for the fruit of His redemption. That's what He earned for you and me. That's the way it should be.

Well, the apostles went to Capernaum. When Jesus was in the house with them, He asked them, "What were you arguing about on the way?" (see Mark 9:33). Here is Jesus. He just got through telling them about coming His Passion. Were they thinking about

His Passion? Were these men wondering and asking questions about what they could do to save Him, or what they could do to be with Him, or how can we pray? I mean, "Let's go to Jerusalem with Him and let's try to save Him." That would be your first thought. "Let's form a guard around Him. Let's do something." Isn't that what you think they would be talking about it? And wouldn't you think one of these disciples would have said to Jesus before His Passion, "What do You mean? I don't understand."

But you know what they did? They put it under the rug and they got very petty and worldly and little. Because they didn't want to face reality. St. Mark tells us, "But they kept silence, for on the way they had discussed which one of them was greatest" (9:34). You know what they were arguing about? First, they said nothing, because they were humiliated. They had put the whole truth and the whole fact about His coming Passion behind them. It was the second time He brought it up, and they put it right behind them; they were arguing about which of them was the greatest. That's all they could think of. Here they were with the Messiah, friends and disciples of the Lord, and all they could think about was which one did He love the most? Whom did He care for most? Which one would be leader? Which one would do this or that? Which one would sit on His right or His left? That's all they could think about.

That's the same with us. You know what happens when we talk about purification or chastisement or anything like that. Some of you change the channel, which is your privilege. Some of you say, "That's crazy." We've had tragedies in the world for years, and so you argue about little things. You concern yourselves with small things like politics or sports, instead of getting your souls together; instead of getting your hearts together; instead of making yourselves repentant; instead of praying the Rosary that Our Lady asked for; instead of praying for peace; instead of getting down on your knees and saying, "Lord God, I have sinned against Heaven and Thee. Have mercy on this world. And if we are at that point where justice is in order, then, Lord God, give me strength and courage, and transform this world that You made so beautiful and we have made so ugly."

We don't do that. We are worried about football games. You say, "Well, Mother, we have to live our lives." I know that. I'm not saying you shouldn't enjoy yourself and go to football games. But I think we're putting the important things not only last, but out of our minds and out of our hearts and out of our sight. The prophecy that Our Lord gave us is later on going to come true: "Death coming like a thief in the night" is going to come true, because you did not see and heed the signs.

So, Jesus sat down with them and He said, "If any man wishes to be first, he shall be last of all, and servant of all" (9:35). He knew of their argument: whom did Jesus love most? How silly, how petty! We do not want to hear that. We want to be served. We want to be first so others can be underneath us. We want to be first so that everybody else is a servant. But the Lord does not think the way we think.

He then took a little child and set him in front of them, and He put his arms around that child. Jesus gave that child a big hug! I want you to picture this child. Jesus just hugged him and He said, "Whoever receives one such little child for My sake, receives Me; and whoever receives Me, receives not Me but Him Who sent Me" (9:36). In other words, give your kids a hug, and if you do that, you welcome Jesus Himself. Anybody you hug, you welcome Jesus, and anyone who welcomes Jesus welcomes the One Who sent Him. You see how deep Jesus gets. He gets very deep—right to the core of the matter. And today there is such a breakup in family. Nobody hugs anybody. Hugging today is almost looked down upon. Although we love, love, love, love everything, we are always suspicious; we have our minds in the wrong place. So, you see, we have lost the concept of pure love because the Lord said if you hug this child you're hugging me. It says here he put his arms around this child. That's what a hug is. You put your arms around someone and you hug them. But He said you are hugging me. Well, you see, my friends, we not only miss signs, we miss the Lord of Signs.

Lord God, I ask that you give us insight and give us the desire to pray. We do not even have, Lord, the desire to pray. You have asked us to pray. Your Mother has asked us to pray, and yet we don't even have a desire to pray because we don't want to see the signs upon us. So, give us a desire to pray. Let us seek the last place, so that we may be servant of all. And we know that whomever we love, if we hug even a little child, we hug You. Amen.

Holy Mary, conceived without sin,
pray for us.
Holy Mother of God,
pray for us.
Mother of Christ,
pray for us.
Mother of Our Savior Crucified,
pray for us.
Mother most sorrowful,
pray for us.
Mother most tearful,
pray for us.
Mother afflicted,
pray for us.
Mother most lonely,
pray for us.
Mother most desolate,
pray for us.

"The Passion of Christ, Prophesied"

Mother pierced by the sword of sorrow,
pray for us.
Queen of Martyrs,
pray for us.
Comfort of the sorrowful,
pray for us.
Helper of the needy,
pray for us.
Protectress of the forsaken,
pray for us.
Support of widows and orphans,
pray for us.
Health of the sick,
pray for us.
Hope of the troubled,
pray for us.
Refuge of sinners,
pray for us.
Hope of the despairing,
pray for us.
Mother of Mercy,
pray for us.
Through your poverty in the stable of Bethlehem,
pray for us.
Through your sorrow at the prophecy of Simeon,
pray for us.
Through your flight into Egypt,
pray for us.
Through your anxiety when seeking your lost Child,
pray for us.
Through your grief when seeing your Divine Son persecuted,
Pray for us.

A Holy Hour with Mother Angelica

Through your fear and anxiety when Jesus was
  apprehended,
pray for us.
Through your pain caused by the treason of Judas and
  the denial of Peter,
pray for us.
Through your meeting with Jesus on the Way of the
  Cross,
pray for us.
Through the tortures of your loving heart in the
  Crucifixion of Jesus,
pray for us.
Through your agony at the death of Jesus,
pray for us.
Through the sword of sorrow that pierced your heart
  when the side of Jesus was pierced by the lance,
pray for us.
Through your deep mourning at His tomb,
pray for us.
Through your desolation after the burial of Christ,
pray for us.
Through the tears you did shed for your beloved Son,
pray for us.
Through the wonderful resignation to the will of God
  that you had to know your sufferings,
pray for us.
Queen of Peace,
pray for us.
In all our tribulations,
pray for us.
In all our illnesses and pain in our sorrows and affliction,
pray for us.

In our need and destitution,
pray for us.
In our fears and dangers,
pray for us.
On the hour of our death,
pray for us.
In the day of judgment,
pray for us.
Lamb of God, Who takes away the sins of the world,
hear us, O Lord.
Lamb of God, Who takes away the sins of the world,
graciously hear us, O Lord,
Lamb of God, Who takes away the sins of the world,
have mercy on us.
Pray for us, O Sorrowful Virgin, that we may be made
    worthy of the promises of Christ.

We beseech You, O Lord Jesus Christ, let Thy Mother, the Blessed Virgin Mary, whose holy soul was pierced by the sword of sorrow at the hour of Thy Passion, implore Thy mercy for us, both now and at the hour of our death, Who livest and reignest, world without end. Amen.

Psalm 22 is the Psalm that Our dear Lord recited on the Cross during the Passion. "My God, my God, why have You abandoned Me?"

You know, it's such an abomination when people think that the Lord was saying that the Father had abandoned Him in total desperation or desolation or despair. That's not what it was. He was merely reciting Psalm 22, which is a Psalm that everybody recited when they were in great pain, in great grief, or in great sorrow. He was doing what every fervent Jew did—He recited Psalm 22.

It says, "I call all day, My God, but You never answer. All night long and I cannot rest. Yet, O Holy One, You who make Your home in the praises of Israel, in You our fathers put their trust. They trusted and You rescued them. They called to You for help and they were saved. They never trusted You in vain."

What Our Lord was saying—what He was admitting—was His total misery before God. You and I must do that often. And then He looked at the Father in perfect trust. The Psalmist continues, "Yet here am I now more worm than man, scorn of mankind, jest of the people, all who see me jeer at me. They toss their heads and sneer."

He relied on Yahweh. The people said, "Let Yahweh save Him. If Yahweh is His friend, let Him rescue Him." That's exactly what they said to Him beneath the Cross. "Yet You drew me out of the womb. You entrusted me to my mother's breasts, placed me on Your lap from my birth, from my mother's womb You have been my God. Do not stand aside. Trouble is near. I have no one to help me. A heard of bulls surrounds me. Strong bulls of Bashan close in around me. Their jaws are agape for me. I am like water draining away. My bones are all disjointed, my heart is like wax melting inside of me. My palate is drier than that potsherd and my tongue is stuck to my jaw...." "I am poured out like water, and all my bones are out of joint: my heart is like wax; it is melted in the midst of my bowels. My strength is dried up like a potsherd; and my tongue cleaveth to my jaws; and Thou hast brought me into the dust of death."

This is the prophecy of the entire Passion of Jesus: "A pack of dogs surround me. A gang of villains closes me in. They are tying me hand and foot, then leave me lying in the dust of death. I can count every one of my bones. Then they glared at me, gloating, and they divided my garments among them and cast lots for my clothes."

This is all in the Scriptures. This entire Psalm was realized on the Cross of Jesus.

This is what was happening on the Cross. *This* is what Jesus did for you. The Psalm says, "Do not stand aside, Yahweh. Oh my strength, come quickly to help me. Rescue my soul from the sword and my dear life from the jaw of the dog. Save me from the lion's mouth. Then, I shall proclaim Your name to my brothers and praise You in the full assembly, for He has not despised nor disdained the poor man in his poverty. He has not hidden His face from him, but answered him when he called. You are the theme of my praise. I performed my vows in the presence of those who fear Him. There the poor will receive as much as they want to eat, and those who seek Yahweh will praise Him. Long life to their hearts, the whole earth, so men do and will remember and come back to Yahweh. And all the families of the nations will bow down before Him, for Yahweh reigns, ruler of nations."

That's what we pray for at the end of our own crucifixion, at the end of the purification of this world in which we live. We can say this prayer. The whole earth from end to end will remember and come back to Yahweh, for Yahweh will reign as ruler of nations. "Before Him all the powers of the earth will bow down, and before Him all bow, all go down to the dust. And my soul will live in Him, and men will proclaim the Lord for generations to come in His holiness to a people yet unborn. All this shall be done." This is what we pray for. This is what we hope for. This is what Jesus merited for us. He gained a new world for us, a new Church, a new presence, a new hope, a new faith, a new love. We look forward to that day when all men will live together in peace and joy and live together as family.

A little prayer to Our Lady to help those who are victims of all the things that are going on—floods and hurricanes and fears of all kind and loneliness and all the things that are sent to us from above and those sent to us that we endure from our neighbor and from ourselves. We ask the Lord to bless us, to give us the courage and the strength and the hope to endure whatever is to come, to give all those around us that great hope and trust in His infinite love and mercy, that even in the midst of chaos and uncertainty we can be stable and assured because we have a God Who loves us. We have a God Who is powerful; we have a God Who is reigning over this world even though it doesn't seem like that; we have a God Who is soon to destroy the power of Satan and all his cohorts; we have a God Who is going to destroy sin and give us a place to live that is full of love and joy.

May the Lord always reign in your hearts!

God bless you.

Chapter 25

"An Hour of Seeking Jesus"

We want to look at Jesus. He's the One at Whom we must always look, and not only look *at*, but look *for*. How often do we look for Jesus?

We look for honor. We look for glory. We look for pleasure. We look for good food. We look for good places to go for our recreation. But do we look for Jesus? Do we seek Him? The Lord said, "Ask. Seek. Knock." So, there is a kind of persistence required in our quest for God.

Most of us are like wildflowers, I think. We just kind of grow. We expect the rain and the sun and the storms. We expect life, we expect death, and that's about it. But do we seek the Lord? You say, "Well, the Lord knows where I am. He knows what's going on in my life. So why should I seek Him?" You *must* seek Him!

You know, one of the problems with married life today and life between families—parents, children, aunts, uncles, grandparents—is that we do not seek each other. We don't want to be together. That's why we have lost the concept of it, the whole idea of family. Our idea of family is that we happen to be cut from the same loaf of bread. That's it. We may get together once in a while on a holiday, but we all want to go our own way. We don't want any interference. We don't want anybody to bother us. We have an aloneness. We're kind of like little hermits. There is a necessity in our lives to be alone and to be on our own. But I don't think you have to throw away the whole reality of seeking each other out. If you don't seek God—if you are not looking for God in the present moment in your life—in your neighborhood events—then I doubt very much that you are going to be seeking your neighbor or wanting, looking for, and desiring family life.

The Trinity is a family. Our life, whether it's our social life, our working life, our family life—whatever life it is that we are living at this moment—has to be God oriented. You say, "Well, I am a lay person, I'm an executive, I'm a dentist and I drill teeth all day. That doesn't matter if you drill teeth, if you're an executive, or if you are a housewife. In everything we do, whether we eat or sleep or drink, there must be that element of God within us: God within you, and God within the event. We're not asking everybody to be monastic nuns and monks. But you are called to holiness just as much as any person of religious life. Many of you are married, so you live a sacrament. A priest lives a sacrament. I don't live a sacrament; religious life is not a sacrament. But it is a transforming life. And so, we need to have our goals.

We're not a God-seeking people today. We want to be on our own. We want to be alienated really from any dependence upon a higher power. We want to be the higher power, and we are just going in circles.

So, we should ask ourselves what it is of which we need to repent, and I think what we need to repent of is the fact that we do not seek the Lord, we do not look for Jesus.

I have a very dear friend who is very close to Jesus. She asked the Lord one day, "What do You want me to do today? What do You want me to do *for You?*" And the Lord said, "Talk to Me."

You know, to us it's unbelievable that God—with all His angels and saints and His Father and the Spirit—would want you and me to talk to Him. You say, "I won't get an answer." Well, you will not if you never speak to Him! You see, this isn't a relationship because we are not seeking God, and that is why we are so blind. Sometimes, in the present, we are blind to truth, and we are not sensitive to error and deception. We are being deceived every day. We are being deceived by people who keep promising everything in this life but nothing in the next. Oh, you're going to get something in the next, you can be sure. It will either be eternal happiness or eternal misery. It will be too late at the end if you've listened to the deceivers. If you make a bad decision when you are dying, it's forever. It's eternal. No change.

So let's ask ourselves, "Do I seek the Lord?" If so, "Do I only seek Him when I am in trouble, or having a real problem?" That's not seeking the Lord. To seek the Lord is to want to be with Him; to want to speak with Him; to want to love Him; to want to be in His presence. The first thing that happens when you begin to love anybody is that you want to be in their presence. That's part of loving. If you can't travel hundreds of miles to go see them, you use the telephone. Why? You want to be in their presence, or at least you want to hear their voice.

How many of you have pictures of your great-grandmother or your grandmother, or your mother and father? Pictures are something to remind us of their presence. We do it all the time with loved ones, and yet we seem to put God out on the fringe somewhere. He made you a person, a human being with an immortal soul, filled with the power of the Spirit and the grace of God!

Now, grace is not a thing; grace is a Person — is the very God Himself dwelling in me. God *dwells in you* if you are in a state of grace. If we have not shoved God out of our lives, God dwells *within us*. We need to seek God, in order to stay in sanctifying grace. Confession — oh, my golly. This is an age when *everybody* needs to go to Confession. Some people ought to go to Confession twice a week, not out of scrupulosity, but because we are not attuned to occasions of sin and how we place ourselves in those occasions that we fall. We don't even admit we have committed a sin. We don't even know the definition of sin. And today, if you even talk *about* sin, you are considered old-fashioned. But God is not old-fashioned. There *is* sin—and sin that is deadly. You can commit it, and anybody who tells you it's not possible is a liar. We have to understand that. Sure, we talk about the compassion and mercy of God. He is merciful: if He weren't, I think He'd have blown us off the face of the earth long ago. But you do not tempt God's mercy. We need to understand that "I was created by God, for God, to be with Him forever." You can flit around in all your cars and your boats and all your pleasures and getting distracted, loving and hating. It's all part of human life. But these should not distract you from the reason you were born—the reason you were created. And that reason is *to know Him, to love Him, and to serve Him in His Church, and in your neighbor.* If we are not doing this, we need to seek the Lord and say, "Lord, I want to find You. I don't know where You are."

Be humble, be honest. Don't put on some big act with God. I mean, He knows you better than you know yourself. So say to Him, "Lord, I don't know You but I want to. Lord, I am a poor sinner. I want to repent but I don't even know how to go about it. I want to be sorry but I've never said that I'm sorry. Please give me the grace to say, 'Lord, I am sorry.' I want to knock on the door of Your heart. I want to ask for forgiveness and love and peace. I want to live in peace. I want serenity of soul. I want to dump my whole life in Your lap—my faults, my weaknesses, my imperfections, my frailties, all of my sins. I want to take just the whole rotten bunch and I want to just dump it in your lap and say, 'Lord, I can't do anything with these. I'm a mess. Please, help me. You do something.'"

Sit there and let Him love you; let Him forgive you. Give Him the opportunity to speak to you in your heart. But you have to speak to Him. You must want God. Some of you never seek the Lord until you are so far down the ladder that there's no way out, and only then do you seek God. Well, that's better than nothing.

So, please, let us ask the Lord not only to give each of us a repentant heart, but to give us a heart that is humble enough to seek repentance, to say we are sorry, to ask, to seek, and to knock.

> Lord Jesus, You gave Your life for us. Teach us how to be repentant. Teach us how to be sorry. Give us a sensitive conscience so that we see and recognize evil before we get too near to it. Give us the grace so we can turn around and turn back. Let us seek You. Give us the grace to ask for forgiveness, to seek Your mercy and to knock at the door of Your heart, that we may rise above the things of this world and arrive at that kind of holiness You desire for us, Lord Jesus, that we may give honor and glory to the Father in the power of His Spirit. Amen.

In the Gospel of St. Mark, the disciples rebuked those who brought children to Jesus. You know, they had a lack of patience. They said get rid of all those kids! The Lord said no, "and said to them, 'Let the little children come to Me, and do not hinder them, for of such is the Kingdom of God'" (Mark 10:14).

Well, *they had it.* You know they did. The Lord kept pounding at them—one thing after another, none of which they wanted to hear. So, by the time you get to Mark 10:32, they were on the road going up to Jerusalem. Jesus was walking on ahead of them, and the apostles were in in a daze, feeling a bit apprehensive. They wanted some good news. It was one of those days when they did not get much good news, though—or, not good to *their* ears. And that's the problem. In truth, it is all good news. But we have itching ears, and the news we want to hear is the news that brings health, wealth, and wisdom. But worldly wisdom is not God's wisdom. So we can understand why these apostles were dazed and apprehensive. They were beginning to think, "Who is going to be saved?" Do you think Jesus relents and just says what they want to hear? No way! Once more, He took the apostles aside and began to tell them what was going to happen to Him. You know, you might look at this and think, "Well Lord, Your sense of timing is a little off. These men are already apprehensive and they are already dazed, and confused. Why don't You wait until tomorrow morning? A good night's sleep will make everything better." But Jesus tells them again: now that they are going up to Jerusalem, the Son of Man is about to be handed over to the chief priests and the scribes, and they will condemn Him to death, hand Him over to pagans, mock Him, spit on Him, scourge Him, and put Him to death; and in three days, He shall rise. Jesus told them every single thing that was going to happen to Him. He gives them hope. He says He will rise. And you know where it went? Right over their heads.

You and I are told the same thing, and it goes right over our heads, too. We have not learned anything. We know that the sufferings of this world are not worthy to be compared to the glory that is to come, but we want glory here. We want it now. We are not worried about the other life. And Jesus told them He would be condemned, handed over, mocked, spit upon, scourged, put to death. Not one apostle heard the fact that, after three days, He would rise again. You know what's so strange about this? The Pharisees heard it! When Jesus was crucified, the Pharisees sent soldiers to the tomb and said, "Hey, you know, this man said He would rise again." But the apostles might as well have had a block between their ears. See how we run from any concept of purification, any concept of suffering, any concept of pain, any concept of God pruning us so that we can become like Him? We run from anything that makes us realize that unless the seed falls to the ground and dies, it remains alone. We don't want to hear that. We want the fruit. We want the tree with no effort.

Well, that's a good way to get nowhere fast, because it's not going to happen that way. I want you to see how ingrained we all are in the desire for the glory and not the pain. And wouldn't you think that these men would have been so sorry? Maybe they took Our Lord aside and said, "Lord what are we going to do when You're spit upon? What can we do to help? And what are we going to do when You're not with us? And, what will we do when You die?"

If I loved someone dearly, as they must have loved the Lord, and I knew in just a few days he was going to be so humiliated and in such terrible pain, but that he would rise, I would have asked those things. I think I would have, but maybe not. You would think that the natural thing when you love someone deeply would be to say, "What are we to do about this? What are we to do, Lord, if this is something that has to be done to save us? Then tell us, Lord, how we can bolster our spirits and keep our courage up."

Did that happen? No. James and John, the sons of Zebedee, came along and said, "Master, we want You to do us a favor." No sympathy at all *for Jesus*! Jesus says, "What is it you want Me to do for you?" And they replied, "Lord, allow us to sit one on Your right and one on Your left in Your glory." Ah, they understood the glory! All they were interested in was one on the right and one on the left.

You can hardly believe this when you read it. But we do the same thing today. We have so watered down the Gospels, we have so watered down the Word of Jesus that we have made it look like a course in positive thinking, that it is about whatever you want to get from it, and that's it. We are told by society, "You are masters of your fate. And God is just some Being Who looks down and blesses us at some point." We don't want to hear the prophecy in our lives that we are going to have to suffer. We don't want to hear about chastisement. We don't want to hear that the Lord has to purify this world so that it can be a world again that we can live in and love and be at peace, and be safe.

Now, we want all of that — love and peace, without pain and suffering. We want to mar our bodies, we want to destroy our souls, and then we expect some magical thing to happen. But we must go through our own passion. We just can't seek the glory without earning it. The Lord says to Zebedee's sons, "You don't know what you are asking for." He asks them, "Can you drink the cup I am going to drink?" Suffering is a baptism, it's a purification. It takes away the disfigurement of our souls. Jesus asks them, "Can you take the baptism of which I am to be baptized?" They said, "We can," and He said, "The cup I will drink, you shall drink, and the baptism with which I am to be baptized you shall be baptized with."

What does this say to you and me? It says that you are going to suffer, Sweetheart, because there is no other way. We are going to be purified because there is no other way. I am going to be purified — you are, the world is, the country is. There is no other way. And then He said, "But to give you a position on the right or the left is not for Me to give." It's already been allotted.

Then He tells the apostles to be careful. Why? Because they are all indignant. Do you understand that these men do not accept the Passion—the necessity of the Passion? Now they are arguing with each other because James and John asked. It was jealousy, plain and unadulterated green-eyed jealousy. At that moment when they should have consoled Him, when they should have been sympathetic and compassionate toward Jesus, were angling for position. He had to correct them, and He said, "Don't let this happen in your midst. For whomever of you wants to be higher than the other, will have to be humble. Whomever of you wants to be the greatest is going to have to be the least."

Well, obviously, even then they didn't catch on. It was only after the Spirit came that they got the light. So if you don't have the light yet, and you're rebelling against the Lord's action and purification in your life, pray that you may get something greater for all eternity.

Pray to the Spirit. Pray to Mary, Our Mother. Ask her to intercede for you. She understood and she stood by Him during the whole Passion. She had faith that He would rise again. Ask Our Lady to help you. She is nature's solitary boast. She is the greatest woman God ever created. She is the masterpiece of the Trinity. Go to Mary. She'll help you understand.

Lord God, give us the grace to know You, to love You, to serve You, to accept from Your hand whatever comes to us, with love, knowing eye has not seen, nor ear heard, nor has it entered our hearts, what You have prepared for us. Amen.

Holy Mary,
pray for us.
Holy Virgin, sprung from the race of David,
pray for us.
Holy Virgin of the root of Jesse,
pray for us.
Holy Virgin, conceived without original sin,
pray for us.
Holy Virgin, presented in childhood in the temple,
pray for us.
Holy Virgin, espoused of the just Joseph,
pray for us.
Holy Virgin, bound by an inviolable vow of chastity,
pray for us.
Holy Virgin, gloriously saluted by the angel,
pray for us.

A Holy Hour with Mother Angelica

Holy Virgin, full of grace,
pray for us.
Holy Virgin, blessed among all women,
pray for us.
Holy Virgin, consenting to the plea of Heaven,
pray for us.
Holy Virgin, conceived by the work of the Holy Spirit,
pray for us.
Holy Virgin, bearing in thy womb the God-Man,
pray for us.
Holy Virgin, Mother of the Lord,
pray for us.
Holy Virgin, Mother of the True Solomon,
pray for us.
Holy Virgin, Mother of God,
pray for us.
Holy Virgin, visiting your cousin Elizabeth,
pray for us.
Holy Virgin, journeying to Bethlehem with thy spouse,
  Joseph,
pray for us.
Holy Virgin, keeping the feasts prescribed by the Law,
pray for us.
Holy Virgin, afflicted by the loss of thy Child when He
  was twelve years old,
pray for us.
Holy Virgin, following thy Son in His ministry,
pray for us.
Holy Virgin, sharing the sorrows of thy Son,
pray for us.
Holy Virgin, standing at the foot of the Cross,
pray for us.

Holy Virgin, confided by thy Son to John, the beloved
   disciple,
pray for us.
Holy Virgin, pierced with the sword of sorrow,
pray for us.
Holy Virgin, Assumed by thy Son into Heaven,
pray for us.
Holy Virgin, reigning in Heaven as Queen,
pray for us.
Holy Virgin, called blessed by all generations,
pray for us.
Lamb of God, Who takes away the sins of the world,
spare us, O Lord.
Lamb of God, Who takes away the sins of the world,
graciously hear us, O Lord.
Lamb of God, Who takes away the sins of the world,
have mercy on us.
Pray for us, O Holy Mother of God,
make us worthy of the promises of Christ.

Let us pray. Protect, O Lord, Your servants by Your abundant
grace, and grant that our confidence in the protection of the
Blessed Mary, Ever-Virgin, and by our humble imitation of
her holy life, may obtain for us security against all enemies
and all dangers, through Jesus Christ Our Lord. Amen.

Psalm 106 says, "Give thanks to Yahweh for He is good, and
His love is everlasting. Who can count all His triumphs? Who
could praise Him enough? Happy are we, if we exercise justice
and constantly practice virtue. Yahweh, remember me for the love
You bear Your people. Come to me as a Savior. Let me share the
happiness of Your chosen ones and the joy of Your nation and take
pride in being one of Your heirs. We have sinned quite as much

as our fathers. We have been wicked. We are guilty. Our ancestors never grasped the meaning of your marvels."

When we say this Psalm, and any other Psalm, we've got to put ourselves into it.

It's not just some old man in the past saying something to God. It's you and me. "They failed to appreciate Your great love and they defiled the Most High. And, for the sake of His Name, He saved them to demonstrate His power." That's what we ask God to do today—to save us by demonstrating His power over evil. One word from Him dried up the Red Sea, led them across the sea as if across dry land. This water swallowed up their oppressors. Not one was left. But they forgot His achievements quickly. Going on before asking His advice, their desires overcame them in the desert and they challenged God in the wild.

We do that today. We are challenging God. You remember when you were a kid—you would draw a line between you and somebody, and you'd say, "Cross that line, put your foot on that line, and see what's going to happen to you." I think sometimes our pride has gotten to a point that that's what we are doing to God today. We are just going over that line to see what He's going to do. And if He doesn't respond right away, we say, "Oh, He's not going to do anything." We are presumptuous. And that's what they did in the past. They forgot His achievements and they grew jealous of Moses and Aaron, Yahweh's holy ones.

You know, it amazes me that we can be jealous of God's holy ones. It's an amazing phenomenon. It just seems to me that we never learn, we really don't! God was going to put an end to sinners if Moses, His Chosen One, hadn't interceded. And, you know, that's true of Mary, Our Mother. If Mary had not interceded for us all these years, if people hadn't been saying the Rosary for years now, I am positive that the hand of God would have struck us down long ago. But He is patient.

There will come a day. So they enraged Him at the waters of Meribah. But, as a result, things went wrong with Moses. Since they had embittered his spirit, he spoke without stopping to think.

In today's world, I just wonder sometimes if we are not in the same boat: we speak without stopping to think what we are saying to the Lord. You know, I hope that's not the case all the time, but we become so presumptuous and we take His mercy for granted, we take His love for granted, we take His patience for granted, it is as if we are almost trying to cross that line to see how far we can go.

You know, it just dawned on me today, that this is really the most Luciferian of sins. It means "I will not serve. I am as great as You are, or greater, and You have no right to tell me I can do this or I cannot do this."

We wish the grace of God to be upon us so that we can, with that grace, with that living, loving presence, be more and more like Jesus every day of our lives. That's why we were born, that's why we are here.

Chapter 26

"An Hour with the King of Kings"

Who is your Sovereign Lord? Who is your King?

You say, "Well we don't have kings anymore. We do have 'leaders.'"

But we still have a King Who is the King of Kings. Are the Father, the Son, and the Spirit — is the One Triune God — sovereign in your life? Is He your leader and your King? If you're a Christian, this is what you should say: "Yes. He is my leader. He is my King. He is my Savior. He is my Lord."

And that is so important because the great sin of today is saying, "I will not serve." I call it the Luciferian sin because it was the first sin ever committed, and it was committed by one of the angels. Lucifer said, "I will not serve. If the Son of God is to be human incarnate, made man, I will not serve Him; He will not be my King." That is exactly why Lucifer and all those angels fell; one-third of the angelic host fell.

Now, a lot of people are telling you there is no such thing as Hell. Do not pay them any attention. They are liars. There *is* a Hell. There *is* a Purgatory. There *is* a Heaven. There *is* a God. There *is* a head of the Catholic Church; that head is the Holy Father; and that head is infallible.

As a Catholic, I am speaking both to Catholics and to those who are not Catholic. Who is your Lord? Who is your King? How many times have you and I said, "I will not serve" when I am disobedient? When I am rebellious? We have tremendous rebellion in the Church today. We say, "I will not serve. I am as good as you are. I am as important as you are," so we have no authority figure because we are each our own authority.

We do not recognize any authority above our own. To say "I am equal" is the Luciferian sin. Lucifer said to God, "I am Your equal. I shall ascend to the throne of God." And St. Michael came up and said, "Who is like unto God?" In other words, Michael said that God has every right to do as He pleases.

How many times have you and I rebelled against that? We don't pay any attention to the Holy Father. We don't pay attention to anyone who has authority. Even the Commandments were changed in a CCD book I read once. It said, "You are going to be good to your parents." What does that mean? "Obey" is the key word that's missing, and obedience is being taken in some texts out of the very Commandments that the Lord God gave us. I do not know about you, but I can tell you Whose side I am on. I am with the Holy Father. I am with the Magisterium. I do not care who knows it, I do not care who likes it. And I think you are going to have to make a choice, too.

I think that you and I ought to repent tonight—repent from the bottom of our hearts for being a rebellious people, a disobedient people. Well, maybe you have not been rebellious, maybe you have been faithful. But we belong to a world that is disobedient. We are members of a world that is unfaithful, and when the chastisement comes (and it will at some time), the Lord is not going to just pick out a few; we are all going to suffer. All are going to have to repent. We are all going to have to bend the knee to the Lord Jesus. We all have to say, "You were right Lord, and I was wrong." If you have a hard time saying it now, are you sure you are going to be able to say it when the time comes?

Lord God, I repent for all the times I have been disobedient to You, to Your Church, to the Holy Father, to the truths in Your Church. I ask pardon for the times I have been rebellious to my parents, to my brothers, to my sisters, to my family, to my coworkers, to my neighbors; the times I have been rebellious against my nation, against the world. The times I have so insisted upon my own way, upon my own will, that have clouded the minds of others and made them confused. Lord God, forgive us our sins, for in committing them, we have drawn You down to the level of an equal, and we have forgotten that there is only one God, Divine and Holy, and we are weak human beings whose pride is surpassed only by that pride possessed by God's enemy. We ask pardon, Lord, for our pride, our rebellious pride, and I pray that those who are faithful remain faithful no matter what; that those who know Thee, love Thee, and serve Thee, will continue on the way of truth and goodness. I ask this in the name of Jesus, through the wondrous intercession of Mary, Our Mother. Amen.

In the eighteen chapter of St. John's Gospel, Pilate went back into the Praetorium as Jesus was beginning His Passion, and called Jesus to him. Pilate said, "Art Thou the King of the Jews?" And Jesus replied, "Dost thou say this of thyself, or have others told thee of Me?"

Have you ever been asked that question? Is Jesus your King?

And Pilate said, "Am I a Jew? Thy own people and the chief priests have delivered Thee to me. What hast Thou done?"

So Jesus replied but He never said what He had done. He answered Pilate's first question, "Are you a king?"

Jesus replied, "My Kingdom is not of this world. If My Kingdom were of this world, My followers would have fought that I might not be delivered to the Jews. But, as it is, My Kingdom is not here." So Pilate said, "Thou art then a king?" And, Jesus said, "Thou sayest it; I am a King. This is why I was born, and why I have come into the world, to bear witness to the truth. Everyone who is of the truth hears My voice" (John 18:33–37).

This is one of the reasons why that terrible movie, *The Last Temptation of Christ*, is such an abomination to God. Jesus said, "I am a King." One of the saddest things in the world today that He is not considered a King, He is considered a man like every other man—or not even that. There are many holy men in this world. There are many holy priests and religious. But He is not even considered one of them. He is depicted as the most depraved kind of man in this world today—an equal. You know, that is what people do with the Holy Father. They say "Hey, you know, we are equals." Once you take the authority from God from your life, then I can guarantee that you are on your way out and on the way down. It may give you a feeling of power for a short time, but the humble Jesus alone is King.

I would like to ask you, and my own soul, a question. If God is King in my life—if Jesus is King in my life, and He founded this Church—then why am I disobedient? That is a very simple question. But if you say, "I don't like what the Church teaches," or "I don't like what the Church is saying," or "I am an equal," then I think you have a problem, a very severe problem of disobedience. Jesus never said that we were going to like everything that the Church teaches. In fact, He used one little parable to tell us this. He said, "A man had two sons, and he went out and asked both to go to the field, and one said yes but he never went. The other said no, but finally he repented and went" (Matthew 21:28–30).

I am asking all of us in this country today: let us stand before God in a humble attitude and know that God has the right to put someone over us, and that our faith must yield obedience. We are so cocky and so proud, and we keep saying, "I am as good as he is;

I am an equal with him; I have my opinion and my opinion is different than his opinion, and our country is different than any other country," and all that gibberish. You see, the Ten Commandments and the Church are for everybody and for every country. We may have different ways of putting them into practice, but the truth can never be changed.

We don't understand kingship anymore. Most of all, we don't understand authority. You know what the sad thing is? Those who will not be obedient cannot command obedience. It follows one from the other. If you are disobedient to God and you are disobedient to the Church, chances are, your children and those who work for you will be equally disobedient to you. Why? Because your example is louder than your words. What you are saying is, "There is no infallibility in the Holy Father because I alone am infallible," but you prove fallibility by your disobedience. Jesus is not your Sovereign Lord. And I think the same thing is happening today as happened in this Gospel passage.

As Jesus told Pilate: "I am a King. This is why I was born, and why I have come into the world, to bear witness to the truth. Everyone who is of the truth hears My voice" (John 18:37).

Where is the voice of Christ today? In His Vicar, the Vicar of Christ, is the voice of Jesus today. All who are on the side of truth, listen to His voice! If you want to know what is happening in the Church today and you want to know what is happening in the world and society and your family, listen to God. Society is not listening to the voice of truth. If you don't listen to the voice of truth, then you only listen to one other voice, and that is your own.

"Pilate said to Him, 'What is truth?'" (John 18:38).

You know what is so sad about that sentence? We do not know what truth is today, because everybody is singing a different tune. Everybody's singing a different song. Everybody is saying something different. The Ten Commandments are only the commandments in this church, in this place. But they are very different in that church, in that place. Do you see what happens when you don't cling to truth and you don't cling to the Magisterium? when the Holy Father is considered an equal and there is no real authority that comes from God Himself? That authority is the essence of the Catholic Church. We have a teaching authority that comes from Jesus Himself and from the Holy Spirit. You can't have a thousand Holy Spirits—there is only One.

I'll bet you are asking yourself the same question: "What is truth?" Who is going to tell me the truth? When a Church such as ours or a nation such as ours, to whom God has been so good, no longer lives by truth but by lies, it goes on to make abortion a law, for example, we do not live by truth anymore. We live by lies, and this is what's so bad today, you see.

When you go to bed tonight, see if you're asking yourself the same question. What is true? You don't worry. You have the sources of truth: the Vicar of Christ is still the source of truth, the Magisterium, the bishops in union with the Bishop of Rome—these are our source for truth. There are no two ways about it. Do not be confused by anyone who does not know truth from air. You can always get what the Holy Father is saying—you can always get the truth. Do not pay heed to those who with their lying lips would lead you astray.

When Pilate said, "I find no guilt in him," he was afraid of the anger of the crowds. He continued: "You have a custom that I should release someone to you at the Passover," he said. "Do you wish therefore that I release to you the King of the Jews?" You know their reply: "Not this man, but Barabbas!" (John 18:38–40).

When we celebrate the Feast of Christ the King, we need to ask ourselves that final question: "Have I chosen Jesus as my King and the Church as His voice in this age, or have I chosen Barabbas? Do I have itching ears that go from confessor to confessor to confessor until I find one who agrees with me? Am I someone who goes from place to place until I find a truth that fits my permissiveness and promiscuity? Do I want people to say yes to everything I want, so that I have no more guilt and I kill my conscience? Or do I accept authority of Jesus Christ?"

Is Jesus King of your life? If He is, then you will have peace and joy. Obedience will bring you freedom. Obedience to the Holy Father and to the Magisterium will bring you holiness of life. Obedience to the gospel will bring you the peace and love that surpasses our understanding.

Remember, no matter how bad things get, no matter how confused the issues are, you need not be confused. There is still in this world a source of truth and a source of light. Never step out of that light. Never move to the right or to the left. Go straight forward and do not become discouraged. Do not become disheartened. There is a God. There is a Savior. He opens up His arms and His Sacred Heart to you. He is your Sovereign Lord. He is merciful and just and holy, and He waits with open arms for you to come and say, "I repent of my rebellion and my disobedience. I ask, Lord, from the bottom of my heart, that You give me light, that You give light to Your Church, so that we may see our errors, we may see our wrong ways, and we may be led to You in humble obedience, the kind of obedience that is pleasing to You. For You have said, Lord Jesus, 'I have come not to do My own will, but the will of Him Who sent Me.' My food is to do Your will." This is my prayer for you and for my poor soul—that together we may build and renew the Church.

Let us pray the Litany of Christ the King:

Jesus, Who did receive crowns and tribute from the Magi,
may all nations serve Thee, O Lord.
Jesus, Who did rule by love the Holy Family of Nazareth,
may all nations serve Thee, O Lord.

A Holy Hour with Mother Angelica

Jesus, as King Who serves Thy people in the example of
filial obedience,
may all nations serve Thee, O Lord.
Jesus, Who draws to Thy realm the fishermen to be fishers
of men,
may all nations serve Thee, O Lord.
Jesus, Your Kingdom is not of the spirit of this world,
may all nations serve Thee, O Lord.
Jesus, Who are King not of the Jews alone, but of all
creation,
may all nations serve Thee, O Lord.
Jesus, Who was mocked by the little rulers,
may all nations serve Thee, O Lord.
Jesus, Who was crowned with piercing thorns,
may all nations serve Thee, O Lord.
Jesus, Who was nailed to the Cross on Golgotha,
may all nations serve Thee, O Lord.
Jesus, Who did ransom His people by the royal Sacrifice
of Calvary,
may all nations serve Thee, O Lord.
Jesus, Who, in Thy Resurrection, was the firstborn from
the dead,
may all nations serve Thee, O Lord.
Jesus, Who, in Thy glorified body, is risen triumphant,
may all nations serve Thee, O Lord.
Jesus, in Whom are all created things in Heaven and on
earth, visible and invisible,
may all nations serve Thee, O Lord.
Jesus, through Whom all things are reconciled unto the
Father,
may all nations serve Thee, O Lord.

That the peoples of this world may know themselves
   subject to Thee,
we beseech Thee to hear us.
That they may put off their vain glory,
we beseech Thee to hear us.
That they may dispel the evils that laicism has brought
   upon society,
we beseech Thee to hear us.
That they may bow their heads before Thee,
we beseech Thee to hear us.
That they may know Your reign is eternal,
we beseech Thee to hear us.
That they may submit to Your just and gentle rule,
we beseech Thee to hear us.
That they may recognize the pope as Your Vicar on earth,
we beseech Thee to hear us.
That they may freely accept his rule for Your sake,
we beseech Thee to hear us.
That they may know that Your Church cannot die as
   nations die,
we beseech Thee to hear us.
That to You, Christ the King, all things may be restored,
we beseech Thee to hear us.

Almighty, Everlasting God, Who in Thy beloved Son, King
of the whole world, hast willed to restore all things anew;
grant in Thy mercy that all the families of nations, rent
asunder by the wound of sin, may be subjected to His most
gentle rule, Who with Thee lives and reigns, world without
end. Amen.

Let us pray for the consecration of the whole human race to
Jesus Christ the King. We used to say this prayer after Mass on the

A Holy Hour with Mother Angelica

Feast of Christ the King, though many places no longer do say it. Let us pray:

> Most sweet Jesus, Redeemer of the human race, look down upon us humbly prostrate before Thine altar. We are Thine, and Thine we wish to be; but, to be more surely united with Thee, behold each one of us freely consecrates himself today to Thy most Sacred Heart.
>
> Many indeed have never known Thee; many too, despising Thy precepts, have rejected Thee. Have mercy on them all, most merciful Jesus, and draw them to Thy Sacred Heart.
>
> Be Thou King, O Lord, not only of the faithful who have never forsaken Thee, but also of the prodigal children who have abandoned Thee; grant that they may quickly return to Thy Father's house lest they die of wretchedness and hunger.
>
> Be Thou King of those who are deceived by erroneous opinions, or whom discord keeps aloof, and call them back to the harbor of truth and unity of faith, so that there may be but one flock and one Shepherd.
>
> Be Thou King of all those who are still involved in the darkness of idolatry or of Islamism, and refuse not to draw them into the light and Kingdom of God. Turn Thine eyes of mercy towards the children of the race, once Thy chosen people: of old they called down upon themselves the Blood of the Savior; may It now descend upon them a laver of redemption and of life.
>
> Grant, O Lord, to Thy Church assurance of freedom and immunity from harm; give peace and order to all nations, and make the earth resound from pole to pole with one cry: "Praise be to the Divine Heart that wrought our salvation; to it be glory and honor forever." Amen.[7]

---

[7] Pope Pius XI, Quas Primas, 1925.

"An Hour with the King of Kings"

That is our prayer for this Holy Hour. That is my desire for you. You know, this prayer is so powerful because it prays that the Church has assurance of freedom and immunity from harm, assurance of the freedom to bow to God as King and Lord, and the assurance of the freedom of maintaining and retaining the truth and not to buckle to the world and what the world desires; not to succumb to worldly gain, to self-glory, to giving people what they want, when they want, and how they want it. The truth is always there. The truth is in the deposit of faith, in the Church. And we consecrate ourselves to the Lord, knowing that where there is truth, there is light. Where there is not truth, there is despair, discouragement, hatred, and darkness. There is confusion, anxiety, and frustration. So you and I must look to the Lord, knowing that He does have everything in His hands, but He has designed that you and I must also pray and intercede. I am asking you to say this powerful prayer. This powerful prayer is the Rosary. Many of my very good non-Catholic friends even say it. I encourage you as Catholics, if you have forgotten how, to get back to saying it. This is the chain of power through which we can keep the Church from the error and darkness and the lack of faith that seems to be rumbling through it. It will keep nations at peace.

Jesus is the King of my life. It is so hard for people to defend their faith. Sometimes they cannot understand it, or they cannot define their faith, but we can always pray those of us who can't define or defend it in public or otherwise. We can always pray.

There are those who are so broken-hearted over things that are happening in society, in their families, neighborhoods, communities, and in the Church, and I think we can become so disheartened that we lose our reality — our reality is the power of prayer and the power of the Rosary. I was told once by an exorcist that the Rosary and the Hail Mary are so powerful that the enemy cannot stand it. Saying the Rosary is something we as a people need to get back to. That is what Our Lady of Fatima has been asking us to do.

A Holy Hour with Mother Angelica

ometimes, some people's problems are so great that the people become kind of numb. I think we have all gotten to that point where we're just kind of numb, and you know, sometimes when I haven't been able to say a prayer, I have just held a rosary. Maybe it even took me a long time to even to say a Hail Mary because I was either broken-hearted or just so depressed, or more accurately, confused, or whatever it was at the time. If you feel that way, just hold the rosary beads in your hands. Just say, "Sweet Mother, help me, obtain grace for me." She is the Mediatrix of all graces. It is through her that all the graces come to us. So ask her to pour those graces onto us, and ask her to obtain from the Lord the grace we need to persevere. If there is any age in this whole wide world, from the beginning of Adam and Eve to now, wherein we need to say a prayer for perseverance, it is now. We live in an age when various erroneous winds of doctrine make you doubtful and confused. Believe me, by saying this Rosary every day, you are not going to be doubtful and you are not going to be confused, because the Lord Jesus is in His Church, and He promised us that the Church would be with us until Gabriel blows his horn!

Many of you are troubled, many of you are confused, and many of you do have tremendous pain in your life—physical, mental, spiritual—and what I want to say to you is for you to be at peace. Give it all to Jesus. If you put all your burdens on to Him, they are His burdens to take.

Humbly accept whatever burdens you have, and then say, "Lord this is Your burden and mine. Help me carry it. Help me to be holy. Help me to seek holiness every day. Let this cross be a source of growth, a kind of springboard to push me way up there and make me more and more like You, Lord Jesus. And I want You to be Sovereign Lord in my life. I want You, Lord Jesus, to be King of my life. I want to profess before God and man that I believe that Jesus is my Sovereign Lord, the Lord Messiah, the Lord King, and that Pope John Paul II[8] is His Vicar on earth, along with all his successors." To that man, and his successors, we owe our love, our obedience, and our prayers.

God bless you!

---

[8] Now Saint John Paul II.

Chapter 27

"The Lordship of Jesus Christ"

We say Jesus is Lord. We've said it a hundred times, and wonderfully so, because it acknowledges a truth. But is He *my* Lord? Is He your Lord? It's so important. You say so-and-so is president of the United States. But do you respect him enough to say he is *your* president? Does he really amount to something in your heart, in your mind? Jesus is Lord. That's obvious. God is supreme. But we do not always act as if God is supreme in *our lives*. Do we really believe that Jesus is the Son of God? If so, is it reflected in our actions? If we say it but don't live it, then we cannot honestly say that Jesus is Our Lord. On the other hand, when you conduct your life in a way such that His life influences your thoughts, your actions, your home life, your business life, your work life, your social life — your whole being — then it rings true when you say, "He is my Lord."

In the old days, we had kings and lords, and if a servant did not obey his lord, then he could never say, "He is my master." That's why Jesus kept telling us over and over, "For whoever does the will of My Father in Heaven, he is My brother and sister and mother" (see Matthew 12:50). That means that God is the head of family. But in today's society, God is denied this role, which is incredible considering it is the family *He* created. But we have the "'new agers" who say they are each a god. All they know is that they exist. Their words are, of course, empty, because they cannot say they had no beginning nor will never have an end. They had a beginning, at birth, and they will have an end, at death.

Then you have all kinds of other people who want their own little god—a god that does and permits whatever it is they want to do and approves of their actions. Sinners want a compassionate God, the kind of compassion that is doting, that allows you to do anything you want to do as long as you can throw up a title and say "Lord." Well, you see, they have no earthly idea what "Lord" means. "Lord" and "obedience" go together. And you and I, in this day and age, have a hard time with obedience. We really do. We will give our memory to God. Most everybody believes in a supreme being—no matter what denomination they are, even if they are not Christian. Muslims believe in Allah. All Christians believe in God. Most believe in the Holy Trinity. That's our memory. We believe, we recall the book, the Gospel, the Torah, and the rest. And we usually give our intellect to God. That's where faith lives, and that means that our intellect acknowledges that He is Supreme and He is Creator and He has power. That's reasonable. Most people, I would say, even some Christians, stop right there. Some of them can recite the Bible almost chapter by chapter, verse by verse. So, they also give their intellect to God. But there's one other faculty you have that they will not give to God, and that is the will. That's what separates the men from the boys, and that's what Jesus kept saying over and over and over. In our lives, this lack of obedience to God's will is why we need to repent. A saint struggles to live God's will, but even he falls. We all do, because of disobedience. That is why we need to repent. We need to repent of the times in which we have acted as though Jesus is not Our Lord. Oh, we are grateful when He does things for us. He grants our intentions. He heals us. He forgives us. For all of this, we have a semblance of gratitude, but we still do not acknowledge Him as Lord.

Let's make a little act of repentance and look at our lives and see all the sins we have committed. Every sin is an act of disobedience. We have said, "Lord, I want to do my own will, right here, right now. I want this pleasure. I want this or that or the other thing, and I am going to get it—now. I don't care what You think about my decision in this regard." Or perhaps we think, "My God is so compassionate, He does not care what I do."

So, let's repent. He does care. He is compassionate but not permissive. He wants you to be holy as He is holy, and many times we have said no to God—in little things and big things. We don't acknowledge His awesomeness on Sundays. We don't acknowledge His day of rest. We treat Sunday like any other day. We don't acknowledge His power in our lives. We grumble over everything from the weather to our jobs to even life itself. Life today is so expendable. People commit abortions because they don't want to bother with giving birth and raising the child in their womb. They would much rather have a boat or another car or a bigger house. People commit euthanasia because they don't love enough to take care of those God has given them as parents. So we're always in the state not only of confusion, but of disobedience as well.

So, God needs to hear from you and me. He needs to hear us say "Lord, Father, I'm sorry. I am really and truly sorry. Give me light, Lord. Give me light to see where I am disobedient; where I displease You; where I don't acknowledge Your power in my life; where I don't accept Your will in my life; where I am not simple enough or childlike enough. Help me to see when I am unkind and impatient and oversensitive and angry. Help me to see when I am caustic and I hurt my neighbor, Lord. Help me to see myself as I really am and take away the fear of seeing this picture of myself. Don't let me put up this veneer that makes me look one way when, inside, I am full of dead men's bones. Let me understand. Give me light, Lord. If I don't have the light, I am not going to see.

A Holy Hour with Mother Angelica

So, Lord, I want to repent of everything displeasing to You in my life. The things I know about, I am very sorry for; and the things I don't know about — the things I am blind to and can't see, I am sorry for those. Let me empty myself of *me* so I can love *You* with a sincere open mind and open heart."

Lord God, bless us as we participate in this Holy Hour. Give us a new mind and a new heart and a new spirit that we may acknowledge You as Lord of All. That we may disappear and decrease and You may increase. We are sorry for our sins, our weaknesses, our imperfections, our infidelities, the things we have done poorly, the good things we have done at the wrong time, the people we have hurt and those we have not forgiven. Lord, give us a forgiving heart. We ask this in the name of Jesus and through the intercession of Mary, that awesome Holy woman.

We want to ask ourselves again, is Jesus Christ my Lord? And you know, if we were to see what Jesus suffered for us, what He went through for us, I do not know how or why it would be so hard to acknowledge Jesus as Our Lord. Because when somebody does as much as He does just for you, that should increase understanding. You know, you are a very unique individual. There's no one like you — past, present or future. Some people may say, "Well, thank God for that!" Be that as it may, there is no one like you, and there never will be. So God loves you with a special love, with a holy love, with an infinite love. Quite simply, there is no end to His love. And then, as you look in the Gospels, you figure out and say, "Well, He loves me that much and look what He did for me!" Don't consider yourself a pebble on the beach. You're not just a grain of sand on the seashore. You're very special to Jesus. And when He went through all of these things, He would have the experience and would understand what you go through, which all adds up to a big "I love you!" If someone I knew and loved had cancer and I had pity or sympathy, that would be good. It would be even better if I were empathetic, meaning I intuited in my heart the pain they were enduring. But if I were to say to them, "Well, okay. I'll tell you what. I'll take the pain. I'll take that whole cancer and I'll be eaten up with it and you go free and healthy." What would they think of *that*? They'd be so grateful that no matter what I asked them to do, they would do it for me. I would have brought them back to life—given them a new life. Would they turn their back on me and slam the door, and never say another word? No! You would think that would be the essence of ingratitude and would be the last thing on their mind. But we do that all the time with Jesus.

St. Luke's Gospel offers some more light on this topic. We've looked at this chapter earlier in this Holy Hour series, but it bears taking another look, for it shows us all of the things that Jesus did for us. "Now Jesus, full of the Holy Spirit, returned from the Jordan and was led by the Spirit about the desert for forty days being tempted the while by the devil" (Luke 4:1–2). *Led by the Spirit to be tempted for forty days by the devil.* Now a lot of people have misused this passage, and they say that the Gospel says He was tempted. Yes, He was, in all things but sin.

Well, this is how Jesus was tempted—not in the flesh because He was so perfect. We are tempted in the flesh because we are imperfect; we're unholy; we're constantly living in a sinful condition. It's very difficult for us not to sin. So, when we are talking about God—when we are talking about Jesus—we have to be very careful that we never, *ever* attribute the work of Satan to Jesus. Now, He was tempted by Satan, but never led by Satan. That's a big difference.

So let's see in what way Jesus was tempted. It says during that time He ate nothing. At the end, He was very hungry, to say the least! Then the devil said to Him, "Well, now, if you are the Son of God, tell this stone to turn into a loaf of bread" (Luke 4:3). It's not mentioned here in Scripture, but I can imagine that wonderful smell of bread that is baking and your mouth waters and you are about to put butter on the freshly baked bread and just go to town enjoying it. Now, I wouldn't be surprised if the devil just kind of created a little odor of freshly baked bread, to accompany his words. And, then he said, "Look, You can have this. Just turn this stone into that freshly baked bread. After all, if You are the Son of God, why can't You do this? It's a very little thing for You." Jesus never spoke to him, which is a real lesson for us dimwits. He simply quoted Scripture and said, "It is written, 'Not by bread alone shall man live but by every word of God'" (Luke 4:4). Jesus' memory is what was being tempted. He was hungry after forty days of fasting, and the devil conjured up the image and thought of food and created the temptation to create food out of stones, a bizarre miracle, to satisfy Himself. But, He quotes that Scripture passage.

The devil was undaunted, and he next showed Him all the kingdoms of the world and said, "I will give you all this power and the glory of these kingdoms." But Jesus said, "It is written, 'The Lord thy God shalt thou worship, and Him only shalt thou serve'" (Luke 4:7–8). There is only One Who is to be worshipped, and that is Jesus Christ and His Father in the Spirit. Some Christian centers never mention the name of Jesus. Their whole concept of spirituality is the world around them and how they react to it. Cosmic God. That's it. Jesus, Son of God, is not in the picture. They have yielded to today's temptation.

The devil was not satisfied, and he suggested Jesus fling Himself down from the top of the temple and all His angels would come to His rescue. And Jesus said, "It is said, 'Thou shalt not tempt the Lord thy God'" (see Luke 4:12). The devil was tempting Jesus with the sin of presumption—to do some magic by throwing Himself down from such an immense height and all the angels, knowing what a great man He is, would come to His rescue.

The devil, having exhausted all the ways he could think by which to tempt Jesus, left, as the angels who sent by the Father were anxious to minister to the Lord. He was so attached to the Father's will, He did not yield to the devil's strong temptations—in spite of the devil springing them on Him at His weakest moment, after forty days of fasting. To spring free of these temptations, Jesus quoted Scripture and kept His Father's will. He acknowledged His Father's will in all things.

Lord, give us grace today not to be tempted by the enemy beyond our strength. Give us grace always to use the Scriptures as a shield against temptation. A humble heart will hold fast and depend upon You. Mary, guard us and protect us from evil.

Heart of Jesus, Son of the Eternal Father,
have mercy on us.
Heart of Jesus, formed by the Holy Spirit in the womb of
the Virgin Mother,
have mercy on us.
Heart of Jesus, substantially united to the Word of God,
have mercy on us.
Heart of Jesus, of Infinite Majesty,
have mercy on us.
Heart of Jesus, Sacred Temple of God,
have mercy on us.
Heart of Jesus, Tabernacle of the Most High,
have mercy on us.
Heart of Jesus, House of God and Gate of Heaven,
have mercy on us.

A Holy Hour with Mother Angelica

Heart of Jesus, burning furnace of charity,
have mercy on us.
Heart of Jesus, abode of justice and love,
have mercy on us.
Heart of Jesus, full of goodness and love,
have mercy on us.
Heart of Jesus, abyss of all virtues,
have mercy on us.
Heart of Jesus, most worthy of all praise,
have mercy on us.
Heart of Jesus, king and center of all hearts,
have mercy on us.
Heart of Jesus, in whom are all treasures of wisdom
   and knowledge,
have mercy on us.
Heart of Jesus, in whom dwells the fullness of
   divinity,
have mercy on us.
Heart of Jesus, in whom the Father was well pleased,
have mercy on us.
Heart of Jesus, of whose fullness we have all received,
have mercy on us.
Heart of Jesus, desire of the everlasting hills,
have mercy on us.
Heart of Jesus, patient and most merciful,
have mercy on us.
Heart of Jesus, enriching all who invoke Thee,
have mercy on us.
Heart of Jesus, fountain of life and holiness,
have mercy on us.
Heart of Jesus, propitiation for our sins,
have mercy on us.

Heart of Jesus, loaded down with opprobrium,
have mercy on us.
Heart of Jesus, bruised for our offenses,
have mercy on us.
Heart of Jesus, obedient to death,
have mercy on us.
Heart of Jesus, pierced with a lance,
have mercy on us.
Heart of Jesus, source of all consolation,
have mercy on us.
Heart of Jesus, our life and resurrection,
have mercy on us.
Heart of Jesus, our peace and our reconciliation,
have mercy on us.
Heart of Jesus, victim for our sins
have mercy on us.
Heart of Jesus, salvation of those who trust in Thee,
have mercy on us.
Heart of Jesus, hope of those who die in Thee,
have mercy on us.
Heart of Jesus, delight of all the Saints,
have mercy on us.

Jesus, meek and humble of heart.
Make our hearts like to Thine.

Let us pray. Almighty and eternal God, look upon the
Heart of Thy most beloved Son and upon the praises and
satisfaction which He offers Thee in the name of sinners;
and to those who implore Thy mercy, in Thy great goodness, grant forgiveness in the name of the same Jesus Christ,
Thy Son, who livest and reignest with Thee forever and
ever. Amen.

A Holy Hour with Mother Angelica

We have been talking about God being the Lord Jesus. There is only One God, and we need to acknowledge Him, and if we acknowledge that Jesus is Lord, one of the best ways to do this is found in this Psalm 113:2–3. "Blessed be the name of Yahweh henceforth and forever from East to West. Praise be the name of God." That is really acknowledging God as your Lord and saying, "Yahweh, Your glory transcends the Heavens." The Psalmist continues, "His throne is so high, He needs to stoop to see the sky. He raises the poor from the dunghill. He lifts the needy from the dunghill to give them a place with the princes of His people. He settles the barren woman in your house by making her the happy mother of children. Praise the Lord" (113:4–9).

Let's pray the Lord's blessing.

Lord, I praise You and bless You and thank You for being so good to us, for being totally faithful. Keep us ever-faithful to Your Word.

May the Lord God bless you and give you His peace. We pray in the name of the Father, the Son, and the Holy Spirit. Amen.

Let's just say yes to God, and tell Him how much we love Him and want to keep His Word.

Chapter 28

"Praying for Unity"

Unity is so elusive today. We hardly see groups or nations that are unified—having one heart, mind, and soul. Or, who are at least willing to speak to each other.

I wonder sometimes if we even understand unity—and the most important unity, of course, is our union with God. I have to be one with God. If I am not one with God, then certainly, I find it impossible to be one with my neighbor—the key element of oneness between myself and God is love. If there is hatred in my heart, then I have no love or unity with God; and if I lack love and unity with God, I lack love and unity with my neighbor. If you are out of touch with your neighbor or with God, it's time to examine your love. I think we need to repent—as always, we start our Holy Hour with repentance—for our lack of love. In fact, every prayer we say or every hour we spend with God should start with a certain amount of *Mea Culpa*: "My fault, my fault, my most grievous fault." We need to have the kind of attitude that knows that we are sinners with weaknesses and faults, some of which we overcome, and some of which we do not even make the attempt to overcome.

But, most of all, we should examine ourselves in love. How much do I love my neighbor? Who is the neighbor that I love the least? Why is it so hard for me to forgive? Has God not forgiven me so very much? Why does injustice spur me on to hatred instead of a solution? Why do I become a part of the problem in a volatile situation? Why do I permit my emotions to run away with me to the point that I lose contact with God and with reality?

When examining our love, it's important to ask, "Do I really trust God?" You know, trust is a part of love because if I love someone, then I trust them. I neither question their attitude nor do I question their love for me. And so the pure love God wants us to have for Him and our neighbor comes directly from Him, which requires trust. I have to have an open channel for it, and that channel is always kept open by a repentant heart. I must have a repentant heart. Now, there's no need to go around all day long saying "I'm sorry, I'm sorry, I'm sorry." But my attitude and my heart must constantly say to God, "I am sorry, Lord. I love You. I am going to try better." This is not always communicated through spoken words, but it can be conveyed through our attitude.

There is a beautiful verse in Psalm 133 that essentially says how good, how delightful it is for all of us to live together like brothers and sisters (133:1–3). Think of the place where you work, for instance. While we are going to have our differences and we can count on our enemy to bring about all kinds of disturbances, do we make an effort at our place of work to love our neighbor and to establish a family-like atmosphere? Maybe some of us are catalysts for unity, or maybe God wants us to be a decisive instrument of it. Very much like St. Francis. You know, one of the beautiful things about St. Francis was that, when families and cities were feuding with another and killing each other off, he would just walk through the city and meet with the two feuding families, and there would be peace, which seemed an utterly impossible outcome. What do you think won them over? His brilliant words or persuasive logic? No, I think it was his love, the source of his gentle spirit, that convinced them to lay down their arms.

So let's think, as we continue to reflect on unity, in what concrete way you and I can serve as unifiers. Let's ask ourselves, "In my work, in my family, in my community, how do I help everyone get back on track toward unity?"

Lord God, we praise and bless You. We ask that You give each one of us, those of us who are listening and those that are not—people all over the world and in every nation—a sense of the necessity of unity, first with You, Lord Father, and then with each other. We ask that Mary, Our Mother, be with us. Her soul, so pure, so holy, the soul that always said yes to God, had a unity beyond compare. Give us that grace. Amen.

"Let us thank You, Father, for giving us Your Son." What a wonderful gift! It's a good bet to say that not many fathers, if any, would allow their sons to suffer like the Father allowed Jesus to suffer for all of us. And most of us are not even grateful, or we seldom are. So, let's take a moment to say, "Thank You, Father, for Jesus. Thank You for the Holy Spirit. Thank You for Mary, that peerless woman. Thank You for all the saints in Heaven, for the angels, and for all the just on earth. Thank You for everything—for pain, for suffering, for joy, for sorrow." Let us draw everything in our lives together as one as with the mysteries of Rosary—Joyful, Sorrowful, Glorious, and now Luminous; all blend together, and in each one there is an element of the other.

Our whole life, if it's going to be unified, needs to be an act of praise and thanksgiving. This knowledge is beautifully given to us by Jesus Himself and His priestly prayer. The Gospel of St. John recounts Jesus' beautiful prayer for unity: "And raising His eyes to Heaven, He said, 'Father, the hour has come! Glorify Thy Son, that Thy Son may glorify Thee, even as Thou hast given Him power over all flesh, in order that to all Thou hast given Him He may give everlasting life'" (17:1–2). You say, "Well, Jesus is saying that right before His Passion, when He knew what every single element of that Passion would be." But it was the Passion that glorified the Father, and it was Jesus' acceptance that glorified the Father.

Jesus was saying, "Give Me the strength, Lord, to endure this pain, that I may be a light for others in pain — to understand that it is their path to eternal life." He explains it even further: "Now this is everlasting life, that they may know Thee, the only true God, and Him Whom Thou hast sent, Jesus Christ" (17:3). That's the whole essence of eternal life. Once you believe that God is Father and God is Lord of all and Jesus is His Son, that is eternal life. What a wonderful Jesus we have!

That life begins here on earth. As Jesus said, as recounted earlier in St. John's Gospel, "I am the bread of life. Your fathers ate manna in the desert, and have died. This is the bread that comes down from Heaven, so that if anyone eat of it, he will not die. I am the Living Bread that has come down from Heaven. If anyone eat of this Bread, he shall live forever; and the bread that I will give is My Flesh for the life of the world" (John 6:48–51).

"He who eats My Flesh and drinks My Blood has" *what* in him? "Life," Jesus says! And it is only God Who gives life, and it is eternal life. Without God's life in you, you have eternal death — eternal death, not extinction. Eternal death is eternal pain. And that's why the Eucharist is so connected with this prayer, because if you know God and you accept Jesus Christ as Lord and Savior, and you accept that Body and Blood into your body and blood, then you become one, unified with God, Jesus, Father, and Spirit — *then* you have eternal life. Isn't that something! You have eternal life, not eternal death, because you are living in the very love of the Trinity. Otherwise you have death, eternally.

Furthermore, He said, "I have glorified Thee on earth; I have accomplished the work that Thou hast given Me to do. And now, do Thou, Father, glorify Me with Thyself, with the glory that I had with Thee before the world existed" (John 17:4–5). Jesus fulfilled His God-given mission and helped us to do the same by becoming like us. As St. Paul wrote, "Jesus, Who though He was by nature God, did not consider being equal to God a thing to cling to, but emptied Himself, taking the nature of a slave and being made like unto man" (Philippians 2:6–7). So, Jesus put aside that glory and cloaked Himself with our humanity. But now He's saying, "It's time to take that glory back—the same glory that I had before the world ever began."

And then He says, "I have manifested Thy name to the men Whom Thou hast given Me out of the world. They were Thine, and Thou hast given them to Me, and they have kept Thy word" (John 17:6). What humility is in Jesus. He said, "These men were Yours, Father, and You gave them to Me." Everything that Jesus did went back to the Father, and everything we do must go back to Jesus.

Jesus continues. "Now they have learnt that whatever Thou hast given Me is from Thee; because the Words that Thou hast given Me, I have given to them" (John 17:7).

You know, sometimes we just think we're so right. When you hear an intellectual or a theologian or philosopher who calls himself or herself Catholic, whose teaching do they give you? That's the key. Whose teaching is it? Jesus says, "I have given them—all of us—the teaching that You gave Me, Father." Whose teaching do you hear, and whose teaching do you give?

"And they have received them, and have known of a truth that I came forth from Thee, and they have believed that Thou didst send Me" (John 17:8).

This is a personal conversation. Have you ever wanted to hear a conversation between the Trinity, the Father and the Son? Well, here it is.

A Holy Hour with Mother Angelica

And Jesus says:

I pray for them; not for the world do I pray, but for those whom Thou hast given Me, because they are Thine; and all things that are Mine are Thine, and Thine are Mine; and I am glorified in them. And I am no longer in the world, but these are in the world, and I am coming to Thee. Holy Father, keep in Thy name those whom Thou hast given Me, that they may be one even as We are. While I was with them, I kept them in Thy name. Those whom Thou hast given Me I guarded; and not one of them perished except the son of perdition, in order that the Scripture might be fulfilled. But now I am coming to Thee; and these things I speak in the world, in order that they may have my joy made full in themselves. I have given them Thy Word; and the world has hated them, because they are not of the world, even as I am not of the world. I do not pray that Thou take them out of the world, but that Thou keep them from evil. They are not of the world, even as I am not of the world. Sanctify them in truth. Thy Word is truth. Even as Thou hast sent Me into the world, so I also have sent them into the world. And for them I sanctify Myself, that they also may be sanctified in truth. Yet not for these only do I pray, but for those who through their word are to believe in Me, that all may be one, even as Thou, Father, are in Me and I in Thee; that they also may be one in Us, that the world may believe that Thou hast sent Me. (John 17:9–21)

Oh, did you hear that? Some of you are so attached to the world. Unless you have a new car every year; unless you have a bigger and bigger house; unless you have this honor and that ambition; unless you have this office; and unless you have so much money and your stocks are going up; you are not content. And, you know what He just said? He said, "I'm not praying for the world, but for those You have given Me, because they belong to You. And all I have is Yours, and all You have is Mine." Talk about unity! He continued, "And in them I am glorified. I am not in the world any longer, but they are in the world, and I am coming to You, Holy Father. Those You have given Me, be true to Your name so they may be one like Us." He wants you and me to be one, like the Trinity is One.

Have you ever even thought of such a high calling from God? Jesus said, "While I was with them, I kept those You have given Me true to Your name, and I have watched over them, and not one is lost except the one who chose to be lost."

Jesus has given you a teaching like no other. The Father gave Jesus twelve men. He said "I have not lost anyone, except the one who chose." Judas went against God. Hell is a place people choose to go to, and Jesus said, "I lost him only because he chose to be lost. And now I'm coming to You. While I was still in the world, I say these things to share My joy with them and I pass Your Word on to them. The world hates them because they belong to the world no more than I belong to the world."

Does the world hate you? Are you going against the principles of the world, against the morals of the world, against the ideas and goals of the world? If you are, then the world will hate you. And Jesus promised us that. He said that "They no more belong to the world than I do, and so that's why the world hates them." We try so hard to be one with the world. We try so hard to be one with everybody, with our peers and with society and with the craze of the day. You can't even dress the way you want to dress. And you know what He said? Something very strange. He said, "I'm not asking You to remove them from the world, but to protect them from the evil one." Some of you don't even believe there is the evil one, which puts you in a bad spot. You have become so one with the world that you cannot see the forest for the trees. "They do not belong to the world any more than I belong to the world," Jesus said.

Now, He said the same thing in three sentences. You have to ask yourself, why does the Lord kept repeating certain sentences? "Sanctify them in truth," He said. "Your Word is truth and, as You sent me into the world, I have sent them. And for their sake I sanctify Myself so that they may be sanctified, too. And I pray not only for these, but those who, through their words, will believe." I mean, Jesus prayed for you. Isn't that wonderful? Jesus, at this moment in His life, prayed for you and for me: "May they be one."

"And the glory that Thou hast give Me, I have given to them, that they may be one, even as We are one; I in them and Thou in Me; that they may be perfected in unity, and that the world may know that Thou hast sent Me, and that Thou hast loved them even as Thou hast loved Me" (John 17:22–23).

Do you realize how much you are loved by Jesus? You are loved by Jesus in the same way that the Father loves Him. That's our witness. Our witness is that we are so completely one with the Trinity that the world will realize He didn't say no. There's a great difference between knowing a truth and realizing truth. I may see a piece of lemon pie in *Life* magazine, but there's nothing there to compare with tasting a piece of lemon pie. That's the difference between knowing and realizing. Jesus wants the world to realize that He is sent by the Father, and that we are one with Him, and that He loves each one of us the way the Father loves Him. If we really knew and understood that one truth, we would get up each morning jumping out of bed with joy. If we lived by that truth, nothing in life could ever get us depressed or discouraged. And no one would ever take away our joy, because if you are loved by the Father and Jesus loves you the way They love Each Other, what else could possibly matter? If you lost it all, what would it matter? You have Their love. Now you talk about unity—*that's* unity.

Lord God, give us a deep understanding of Your unity—what it means to be loved so much; to be one with Jesus and the Father and the Spirit in me so that I may love my neighbor; that this love will so possess me; that my joy will never leave me; that the world may realize that Jesus is Lord. That is my mission. All else is of little value if I do not preach that sermon. It would be as if I have been mute all my life. Amen.

Let us pray the Litany of the Holy Spirit:

Lord, have mercy on us.
Lord, have mercy on us.
Lord, have mercy on us. God the Father of Heaven,
have mercy on us.
God the Son, Redeemer of the world,
have mercy on us.
God the Holy Spirit,
have mercy on us.
Holy Trinity, One God,
have mercy on us.
Divine Essence, one true God,
have mercy on us.
Spirit of truth and wisdom,
have mercy on us.
Spirit of holiness and justice,
have mercy on us.
Spirit of understanding and counsel,
have mercy on us.
Spirit of love and joy,
have mercy on us.

A Holy Hour with Mother Angelica

Spirit of peace and patience,
have mercy on us.
Spirit of longanimity and meekness,
have mercy on us.
Spirit of benignity and goodness,
have mercy on us.
Love substantial of the Father and the Son,
have mercy on us.
Love and life of saintly souls,
have mercy on us.
Fire ever burning,
have mercy on us.
Living water to quench the thirst of hearts,
have mercy on us.
From all evil,
deliver us, O Holy Spirit.
From all impurity of soul and body,
deliver us, O Holy Spirit.
From all gluttony and sensuality,
deliver us, O Holy Spirit.
From all attachments to the things of the earth,
deliver us, O Holy Spirit.
From all hypocrisy and pretense,
deliver us, O Holy Spirit.
From all imperfections and deliberate faults,
deliver us, O Holy Spirit.
From our own will,
deliver us, O Holy Spirit.
From slander,
deliver us, O Holy Spirit.
From deceiving our neighbors,
deliver us, O Holy Spirit.

From our passions and disorderly appetites,
deliver us, O Holy Spirit.
From our inattentiveness to Thy holy inspirations,
deliver us, O Holy Spirit.
From despising little things,
deliver us, O Holy Spirit.
From debauchery and malice,
deliver us, O Holy Spirit.
From love of comfort and luxury,
deliver us, O Holy Spirit.
From wishing to seek or desire anything other than Thee,
deliver us, O Holy Spirit.
From everything that displeases Thee,
deliver us, O Holy Spirit.
Most loving Father,
forgive us.
Divine Word,
have pity on us.
Holy and divine Spirit,
leave us not until we are in possession of the Divine Essence, Heaven of heavens.
Lamb of God, Who takest away the sins of the world,
send us the divine Consoler.
Lamb of God, Who takest away the sins of the world,
fill us with the gifts of Thy Spirit.
Lamb of God, Who takest away the sins of the world,
make the fruits of the Holy Spirit increase within us.
V. Come, O Holy Spirit, fill the hearts of Thy faithful,
R. And enkindle in them the fire of Thy love.
V. Send forth Thy Spirit and they shall be created,
R. And Thou shalt renew the face of the earth.

A Holy Hour with Mother Angelica

Let us pray. God, Who by the light of the Holy Spirit instructed the hearts of the faithful, grant us by the same Spirit to be truly wise and ever to rejoice in His consolation. Through Jesus Christ Our Lord, Amen.

When praying for unity and while trying to be unified with God and ourselves and our neighbor, there are two things that are very important: thanksgiving and praise. Because in thanking God, I know I owe Him a debt, and that debt is a debt of love. In praising Him, I acknowledge that He is the God of Love. And so, in all my weakness, if I thank and praise God, then I boost myself up over and above my own failings, and that is why we just prayed that the Lord deliver us from all these weaknesses.

In Psalm 116 and 117, we have each a Psalm of praise and thanksgiving. Because I love Him, Yahweh listens to my entreaty and He bends down to listen to me when I call. That's the love of God. That's unity—God united to us. Though we are not always united to Him, He is always one with us. But we have to be one with Him, so He bends down.

"The snares of death encompassed me; the pangs of Sheol laid hold on me; I suffered distress and anguish. Then I called on the name of the Lord: 'O Lord, I beseech Thee, save my life!' Gracious is the Lord, and righteous; our God is merciful" (Psalm 116:3–5).

Some of you think that God is so terrible. Oh, He's unjust and mean and waiting with a baseball bat to whack you on the head every time you blink an eyelash! On the contrary: "The Lord preserves the simple; when I was brought low, He saved me.... I walk before the Lord in the land of the living. I kept my faith, even when I said, 'I am greatly afflicted.' I said in my consternation, 'Men are all a vain hope.' What shall I render to the Lord for all His bounty to me? I will lift up the cup of salvation and call on the name of the Lord. I will pay my vows to the Lord in the presence of all His people" (Psalm 116: 6, 9–14, RSVCE).

Isn't that beautiful? Do we walk in Yahweh's presence and have faith, even when we're completely crushed? Just listen to what the Psalmist, possibly King David, has to say on that score!

Psalm 117, verses one and two, offer more guidance: "Praise the Lord, all nations! Extol Him, all peoples! For great is His steadfast love toward us; and the faithfulness of the Lord endures forever. Praise the Lord!" (RSVCE).

Oh, are we ever far from that ideal! In fact, in the name of God, we kill and we murder. We destroy—all in the name of God. Let us pray for unity in the world, for unity in our country, for the children who are aborted. You know, it's very difficult to know how we can have a unified nation when we are so far away from God—when abortion and murder are acknowledged in the law as righteous, when we take righteousness and so twist it that we don't recognize it. Let us pray for our nation and all nations of the world. Let us pray, as the Scripture invites us, that all nations will, one day, be under God again. Whatever it takes, Lord, let it happen!

Let us pray that you and I may practice the peace and the love of Jesus, and that wherever we go, wherever there's land, there may be peace.

Let us pray to Our Lady, who promised us at Fatima that if we prayed much and prayed the Rosary daily, there would be peace. May peace be in your heart, and the joy of Jesus in your soul continually.

God bless you.

Mother M. Angelica
(1923–2016)

Mother Mary Angelica of the Annunciation was born Rita Antoinette Rizzo on April 20, 1923, in Canton, Ohio. After a difficult childhood, a healing of her recurring stomach ailment led the young Rita on a process of discernment that ended in the Poor Clares of Perpetual Adoration in Cleveland.

Thirteen years later, in 1956, Sister Angelica promised the Lord as she awaited spinal surgery that, if He would permit her to walk again, she would build Him a monastery in the South. In Irondale, Alabama, Mother Angelica's vision took form. Her distinctive approach to teaching the Faith led to parish talks, then pamphlets and books, then radio and television opportunities.

By 1980 the Sisters had converted a garage at the monastery into a rudimentary television studio. EWTN was born. Mother Angelica has been a constant presence on television in the United States and around the world for more than thirty-five years. Innumerable conversions to the Catholic Faith have been attributed to her unique gift for presenting the gospel: joyful but resolute, calming but bracing.

Mother Angelica spent the last years of her life cloistered in the second monastery she founded: Our Lady of the Angels in Hanceville, Alabama, where she and her Nuns dedicated themselves to prayer and adoration of Our Lord in the Most Blessed Sacrament.